HAVE A SEAT, PLEASE

HAVE A SEAT, PLEASE

Don Reid
with John Gurwell

Texas Review Press
Huntsville, Texas

FIRST EDITION, 2001

Requests for permission to reproduce material from this work should be sent to:

Permissions
Texas Review Press
English Department
Sam Houston State University
Huntsville, TX 77341-2146

Cover photography by Richard Nira; photograph of "Old Sparky" courtesy of Texas Prison Museum (Huntsville, Texas)

Cover design by Kellye Sanford

Library of Congress Cataloging-in-Publication Data

Reid, Don, 1906-
    [Eyewitness]
    Have a seat, please / Don Reid with John Gurwell.-- 1st ed.
       p.   cm.
    ISBN 1-881515-33-8
    1. Capital punishment--Texas. 2. Death row--Texas. 3. Death row
inmates--Texas. 4. Executions and executioners--Texas. 5. Reid, Don, 1906-
6. Journalists--Texas--Biography. I. Gurwell, John. II. Title
    HV8699.U5 .R33 2001
    364.66'0092--dc21

                       2001027583

For Patsy Woodall,
whose help and inspiration made me a pretty good
newspaperman. I'm grateful, too, that she gave me an
opportunity to serve, as best I could, my town, my state
and the people . . . .

—Don Reid

Foreword

Few controversies these days are more fervent than the debate over capital punishment; few books offer a more memorable account of a man's soul struggle with the issue than Don Reid's *Have A Seat, Please*, initially published in hardback under the title *Eyewitness*.

It so happened that one day in Brookshires I encountered Nelda Woodall, to whose mother this book is dedicated, and while we were discussing the Reid book, she mentioned that she tried to talk Don into using the title *Have a Seat, Please*, the words the warden used just before the condemned man was seated in the chair and strapped down. (Nelda's folks owned the *Item* when Don worked there; in fact, they hired him.) She said that she always regretted that Don chose the title *Eyewitness*.

I got to thinking about the incredible irony of that last utterance of civility the condemned man would ever hear and decided to give Don Coers a call. Don's the Vice President for Academic Affairs at Angelo State and still maintains a position with the press here, and I trust his judgment on such matters. He agreed with me that the title would appeal to a broad spectrum of readers for different reasons, so we concluded that if Frances, Don's widow, and Kathy Gurwell, whose father assisted Don on the book, would agree to the title change, that's what we would go with. They both liked the idea.

Have a Seat, Please is the chronicle of Don Reid's long period of soul wrestling over the issue of capital punishment. As a witness for the *Item* and the Associated Press over a period of thirty-five years, he watched 189 men die in "Old Sparky." We're talking about a man observing not the slow, methodical administration of capital punishment through lethal injection but the terrifying immediacy of electrocution, with 1800 volts of electricity sent through the condemned, from the electrode attached to the shaved spot on the top of his head to the one attached to his left leg.

Lest you misunderstand, this book is not a parade of graphic descriptions of men being electrocuted; rather, it is the touching story of a man whose attitude toward the death penalty changed very slowly from passive endorsement of the system to almost militant opposition to it and who had a definitive role in bringing about reforms in the parole and rehabilitation systems currently employed by the Texas Department of Criminal Justice. Neither is it a strident condemnation of the system of punishment approved of in those days. Reid takes us through case after case involving men on Death Row, from Albert Lee Hemphill, his first, to Joseph Johnson, his last. He humanizes the condemned in ways that few people have ever tried before, not to drag into question their guilt but to demonstrate that in one way or another every one of them was a unique human being, capable of hope and understanding, and he treats with amazing gentleness and respect the prison authorities responsible for carrying out their mandates.

Many changes have occurred in the Texas Department of Criminal Justice since Don Reid kept his dreadful vigil, most for the better, but the executions continue and the debate goes on, as it likely will until, in William Faulkner's words, "the last ding-dong of doom has clanged and faded from last worthless rock hanging tideless in the last red and dying evening." Even then Don Reid's inexhaustible voice will still be ringing clear.

Paul Ruffin, Director

He that smiteth a man, so that he die,
shall surely be put to death . . . .
—Exodus

Ye have heard that it hath been said,
An eye for an eye, and a tooth for a tooth:
But I say unto you, That ye resist not
evil: but whosoever shall smite thee
on thy right cheeck, turn to him the
other also . . . .
—Matthew

1

The Ritual

Half a century of crime and punishment is tucked away in a drab green filing case in a Department of Corrections office in Huntsville, Texas. Those 50 years represent the life and times of 506 lodgers on Death Row, a majority of whom died in the electric chair to pay for their crimes against the people of the sovereign state.

Some escaped the chair with commutation of their sentences to life imprisonment.

Some were freed because they were falsely imprisoned or improperly tried.

And, in my opinion, some who were innocent were executed.

No one has died in the chair since 1964, but the papers in the filing case continued to pullulate until 1972, when the U.S. Supreme Court ruled the death sentence cruel and unusual punishment and thus unconstitutional. It was cruel and unusual, the Court maintained, because it was meted out in a frivolous and arbitrary manner. In that eight-year period —from 1964 to 1972—juries and courts continued to hand down the death penalty; district attorneys continued to demand it; inmates continued to struggle to escape it.

Now, at the time of this writing, 1973, Texas, other states, and the federal government are attempting to restore forms of capital punishment, trying to tailor them to meet the Court's requirements. It seems likely that the flow of papers into the filing case will resume.

Inside the case at the moment are four smoothly sliding

drawers jammed with official brown envelopes, some thick, some thin, all neatly-numbered from 1 to 506. Within the envelopes are the hopes and fears, pleas and protests of the condemned . . . and the state's objections and rejections. And among these writs, denials, psychiatric reports, criminal records and hand-scrawled confessions and refutations—in each envelope—is a square of white paper. In each case it has been the last document added, the official notice that the ultimate penalty—"Death by Electrocution" —has been assessed. Or, in far fewer instances, that the death sentence has been commuted to life imprisonment.

There is savagery in these bits of paper; they are crimsoned by the most perverted, the most vicious, brutal acts man can visit on his brothers. And there is a bit of dignity, and courage at times; hardly a man is craven all his life. There is wit and humor, too. Grim and bitter, generally—but it is there.

I have thumbed my way through this mounting record for more than 35 years, studying the actions and the personalities of Numbers 1 through 506. I have listened to their stories from their own lips. I have shared their "last meals" on Death Row. I have watched them walk their "last mile" down the corridor and through "the little green door" to sit down and die on the sturdy chair some wryly called "Old Sparky."

The documents rustle with memories. The numbers surface through the mists of my subconscious to remind me of the men whose lives and deaths give a texture of depth to their violence. No. 336 emerges from time to time. That was J.B. Patterson, a middle-aged farmer who deserted his wife and eight children for a big-city Jezebel, then killed the temptress for wrecking his dreams and breaking his heart.

No. 379? Walter Whitaker. The handsome scion of a prominent and wealthy Eastern industrialist who throttled his teenage sweetheart one stormy night in a tragic interruption of an elopement across the high plains of West Texas. Whitaker remembered it all and told the Texas Rangers about it—*after* two lie detector tests had failed to prove him guilty.

No. 334? That was Herman Lee (Humpy) Ross, a 92-pound hunchback as venomous as a cobra. Ross killed a man in a Galveston holdup, escaped jail and killed a detective before he was finally brought to bay. Humpy leaped for my throat at the very instant three husky guards were wrestling him into the electric chair. I shall never forget Humpy Ross!

And Adrian Johnson, one of seven young teenage blacks who were accused of sexually molesting a young white boy, then stuffing him into an abandoned ice box to suffocate and die in terror. Johnson was baptized in prison and died in the chair with the smile of a choir boy on his lips. He was No. 424.

And Morris Addison, No. 381. He told me his story the morning of his execution day, of knifing a white man to death on an Austin used car lot. It had not been told in Court. Then he rubbed a finger along his arm and said: "See that skin? That's why there's no chance for me."

By three o'clock that afternoon, just six hours after I had told the Parole Board Addison's story, his sentence of death had been stayed. Today he is a free and productive member of society.

Numbers? The state has numbers stamped on *all* its property. The drab green filing case has one: No. 11,444.

So has the electric chair. It is an ancient piece of furniture—solid oak, high-backed, sturdy, held together by wooden pegs and festooned with wires and leather straps and electrodes. Convicts themselves, working in the prison carpentry shop, hand-crafted the device half a century ago, and stained it to accentuate and preserve the natural beauty of the grain.

It was first utilized the night of February 8, 1924. In that tune-up for the task to come over the years, five men—Nos. 1 through 5—"went down." They had been stacked up on Death Row awaiting the initial application of the new mode of execution in Texas. The chair carries No. 8,573.

These elements—the chair, the whining generators, the condemned men, their keepers, their cells, their coffee pot, the shower stall, the barber's chair—all are enclosed in a small, one-story red brick building with green doors in the courtyard of the Huntsville unit of the Texas Prison System. This is the Death House.

It is the theatre in which I have played more than a spectator's role in a seemingly endless ritual of death.

I have watched 189 men and boys die as the climax of that ritual.

Death Row is not, physically, an unpleasant place to live. There are eight airy cells, each five feet by ten feet. Each cell has its own cot, toilet, water basin and table. True, the side and rear walls are of solid sheet steel, but they are painted a subdued green and ecru. The front wall, which includes the door, is in reality a barrier of two-inch steel bars.

The open area between the cell fronts and the opposite wall is called "the corridor." It is 45 feet long. At one end, to the right of and in plain view of the prisoners in the cells, squats the barber's chair; at the other end is a green door. Along the corridor wall opposite the cell fronts is a long steel cabinet with shelves for sugar, coffee, soft drinks, tanks of ice water and orange juice. Coffee is brewed atop the cabinet 24 hours a day.

Eight high, narrow windows admit fresh air and illumination from the outside, including brightening rays of the morning sun that do not arrive until they have climbed the 40-foot high prison wall to spill over and into Death Row. The windows open outward from the walls near the ceiling, and protruding from the walls near each are electric fans that agitate the fresh air drawn through the open windows and swoosh it into the cells.

A row of 100-watt light bulbs hang from the ceiling below white porcelain reflectors that scatter illumination into every nook and cranny of Death Row. The "lights out" signal is given at 10 p.m., but prisoners have their own individual reading lights. And they also have earphones for their radios. The men can lie in their bunks and listen to favorite programs all night if they desire.

From their cells, the condemned men can see the barber's chair and watch another Death Row inmate get the crown of his head and his left leg shaved so the electrodes can fit properly and effectively. To the left of the cell doors, not more than 20 steps from the farthest cell, is "the little green door" that leads into the Death Chamber.

Only one condemned man, to my knowledge, ever returned alive after passing through that green door. Just outside the door is the telephone. It rang a reprieve for No. 316—Fred Jones, a Floydada, Texas, supermarket operator—the night Jones stalked reluctantly through the door to confront his oaken nemesis. It was a brief respite; just three days, enough time for authorities to check out a newly-offered but unfounded reason why Jones should not die. Then, Jones went down.

Three guards maintain constant vigil in Death Row, each working an eight-hour shift. One cannot leave his post until he is relieved by the succeeding guard. Indeed, they are locked into Death Row with their wards, completely un-armed except for their physical strength should they ever need to defend themselves. But they are in constant contact with the outside world by telephone, and it with them.

The telephone is all important to the condemned. It announces to the guard that visitors are coming to brighten the day for someone along Death Row. By telephone, the extra wants of the condemned are filled; they make out lists of items and give them to the guard who summons a "runner" to get the orders filled. But there are limitations, naturally. Since the warden cannot have his "building superintendents," as they are officially termed, running to and from Death Row at the beck and call of its lodgers, he requires prisoners to pool their requests for a morning and an evening "run" to the prison commissary.

The telephone will tell a man that his attorney is arriving with important papers for him to sign, papers that may pro-long his life or even spring him from Death Row forever.

It is when the telephone doesn't ring for a man on his execution day that his hope and his faith are put to the severest test, and hope and faith may falter.

The guards also function as waiters, mailmen, newspaper delivery boys (it is just a short paper route) and confidants to their wards. They admit visitors—chaplains, prison officials, attorneys, families and friends and, occasionally, visiting newspapermen who show up mostly around execution time.

In addition to folding chairs, the guards provide visitors with coffee, perhaps a light snack, and make sure they do not violate their own privileges or those of the men they come to see.

Twice daily the guard supervises the distribution of food brought by a rolling wagon and makes sure it contains no utensils that could possibly become a weapon. The condemned are fed twice daily, at 9:30 a.m. and at 5:30 p.m. The state figures they don't burn up much energy.

Physically, then, the condemned men are well cared for. They can order anything within reason from the commissary, or get a chaplain or visitor to fill an order for them, as long as they have the money to pay. Their time is what they make of it, but it must be spent within the confines of their tiny cells. After all, the condemned are not members of the regular prison society, but guests from the Texas counties. The Death House is maintained by the state for the benefit of these counties and their district courts. A county sends a check for $25 to Huntsville along with each man it ships there. The $25 is the fee the state charges for use of its central holding and execution facilities. Obviously, the fee does not begin to cover costs of maintenance. When a sentence is commuted to life, the prisoner is removed from Death Row to join the regular prison population, given a new number, and absorbed into the prison routine.

But emotionally, the condemned man lives in a world of tension. He knows almost to the second when he will die. He sits in his cell and watches others mount the barber's chair for the quick head and leg shave, listens to the water splash as they take their final shower, shares in their last meals, sits mute as friends and family bid tearstained farewells as they huddle in sad little semicircles outside a cell door on the folding chairs provided by the guard.

Condemned men never leave their cells except to

shower or get a haircut, and they cannot mingle with their neighbors on Death Row. Only one inmate at a time may walk the corridor. Occasionally a condemned man's presence is required at a hearing scheduled by his attorney in an effort to gain a commutation of sentence or a new trial. It is, at best, a brief journey into the free world.

Each morning the condemned tick off the remaining days of their lives in bold crosses penciled on red and white calendars supplied for their cells by the state . . . crosses that subtract, day by day, their time on earth until it dwindles down to the few hours that is execution day.

Time runs out and the calendar is taken down from the wall. The name tag is removed from the cell door. A new lodger arrives and *he* is given a new calendar. A new date is circled, a new line of crosses begins to march toward the freshly-circled date.

How does a condemned man spend his final hours?

If he has slept at all, he awakes to silence—unaccustomed silence. He lies on his cot, quickly recognizing that the silence is prompted by his companions' concern for him. No radio plays. No voice hums. No pen scratches paper.

Slowly his head turns on the pillow and his gaze fastens on the calendar. As if this slow movement is a signal, the guard appears at the cell door with a steaming mug of coffee. The final stage of the ritual is beginning.

The condemned man takes the coffee, nods his thanks. As he sips the coffee he lifts a Bible from beneath his cot and opens it. He reads as he sips, retreating into that ancient world with its admonitions and its hopes. He can do this— move out of his time and place. He has taken what the inmates call the "Jesus Route." He has given up all but the slightest vestige of hope of reprieve or commutation, so he has clutched the only hope left. Most condemned men do this, and they are able to hold off their fear in a euphoria created by reading the scriptures and listening to the quiet, insistent voice of the chaplain.

There is a light tap at the cell door. It is the guard. The condemned man rises, slips out of his pajamas, dons white cotton shirt and trousers. A tall white-haired man appears at the cell door.

This is Joe Byrd, assistant warden. Around midnight he will kill the condemned man.

Byrd is a gangling man with a shambling gait whose trousers appear too large for him. He lives with his family in the prison housing complex—in the very shadow of the prison wall.

Byrd has a warrant in his hand. He had picked it up in the warden's office and examined it carefully to make certain the name, date and other particulars were correct. Enroute he had spoken with Father Francis Duffy, the chaplain, his chief ally in the performance of the ritual.

Now Byrd leans forward to peer through the bars at the condemned, who passed his 25th birthday on Death Row. The man waits; Byrd must speak first. It is part of the ritual. The man has learned this from watching others rise to face Joe Byrd.

"Good morning," Byrd says. "How are you today?" His voice is soft, but it rings along the line of cells.

"Hello, Mr. Byrd," the man replies.

They know things about each other, these two. The man knows that this bespectacled, ruddy-faced man with the pale blue eyes has the reputation of being "firm but fair," a man who no doubt has some sympathy for those on Death Row but one who refuses to "put up with any foolishness." A man who lends dignity to the ritual.

Byrd knows the man beat to death an elderly druggist for the contents of his wallet, that he was condemned to die and must die. And that he, Joe Byrd, must carry out that mandate.

Byrd lifts the warrant and begins to read in a strong, clear voice, "It is the mandate of this court that you . . . shall be executed . . . ."

The man is not listening. For the first time he can hear the slight noises his cellmates make as they shift on their cots or rustle a newspaper. He raises his gaze to Byrd's face only when Byrd has finished reading the warrant.

Byrd lowers the paper and asks, "What would you like for dinner?"

Because this is an important part of the ritual, the condemned has given considerable thought to the matter. He has heard others order huge repasts, has heard one inmate ask for watermelon on a wintry day to the confusion of the prison dietician. Steak and strawberry pie topped with whipped cream, once the favorite ritual menu, has given way of late to mountains of fried shrimp.

Silently he hands Byrd a slip of paper through the bars. Byrd studies it and smiles. Fried chicken. Mashed potatoes and gravy. Hot rolls. A large bowl of strawberries (if there are any). And ice cream—five orders. Byrd knows the man will manage to send four of the bowls of ice cream to the others along Death Row.

It is time for Byrd to exit, to make way for Father Duffy. He nods to the approaching priest and heads back to his office for further preparations.

The man in Cell 3 welcomes the priest with a smile and a wave, then turns to retrieve his Bible from his cell cot. The priest's eyes flick over a familiar scene—the huge lock on the cell's barred door, the extra security provided by a heavy link chain looped around the cell door jams and tied together with a padlock.

(The extra lock is a concession to fears of the management that someone, some day, will emulate a feat performed by Raymond Hamilton and Joe Palmer some years earlier. The two were notorious "badmen" of the 1930s, members of the Bonnie Parker and Clyde Barrow gang. Using smuggled automatic pistols to command attention, they broke out of Death Row to freedom, the only successful Death House break recorded in Texas.)

The condemned man moves closer to his cell door. His blue eyes never waver as the priest looks searchingly through the steel bars.

"Do you accept Jesus as your savior, with no reservations?" Father Duffy asks.

"Yes, Father, I do."

The condemned man sinks to his knees and the priest reaches through the bars and places his hand on the convert's head. He baptizes the kneeling man in the Catholic faith, his arm rising and falling as he sprinkles holy water on the wavy black hair. His voice rises strong and clear, penetrating every corner of Death Row.

A throat is cleared in Cell 2 and the guard pours a glass of orange drink and silently passes it through the cell bars.

Father Duffy completes this ritual within a ritual. He reaches through the bars to shake hands with his new convert. He exits. The condemned turns to his cot and soon, open Bible in hand, is absorbed in the scriptures.

Death Row comes alive with the crackle and swish of turning newspaper pages, of muttered comments on the state of the nation as reflected by the black headlines and the finer print beneath them. Even so, the day will remain muted, even to the arrival of the breakfast food wagon with its clatter and clinking of trays and utensils.

The condemned man spends an hour with two visitors, friends who draw smiles with their description of the details of their trip from the reception room through the doors and gates and courtyards to the Death House. He accepts their self-conscious and sometimes stumbling words of sympathy and regret with silent nods or brief words of thanks, then gravely shakes hands with each as they arise from their chairs to depart; he had asked the guard to limit their visit to as brief a period as possible.

The next hour is spent in almost stilted banter with his Death Row mates, whom he had seen only briefly as they passed his door to and from the shower or as they sat in the barber's chair for a haircut. But he knows their voices.

"You gonna make it okay," says the man two cells down. "I know you will, and God will be with you."

"I hope you ordered a big dinner," comes a drawling voice from Cell 2. "Not that I'm trying to beat you out of any of it . . . ."

Chuckles edge from cell doors, and the guard recalls the time when the cook questioned a "last meal" menu that included five slices of chocolate cake until he remembered there were five men on Death Row. He had sent along an entire cake.

The brisk ring of the telephone brings complete silence

along the corridor. The guard talks briefly, then announces that a newsman is coming on Death Row later to eat the "last meal" with the condemned man. Conversation slowly resumes.

The newsman arrives. He waves a friendly hand at the inmates, says his "hellos," and accepts a soft drink from the guard. He picks up a chair and continues on to Cell 3. "What do you know that's good?" he asks the man as he places his chair and sits down.

The man shows him a wry grin. So the newsman gives him the "word." The Parole Board has turned down a last plea for clemency. He watches the man closely. Father Duffy has told him that the man was in an excellent frame of mind in the morning—and had been converted. He sees that the bad news does not unduly perturb the condemned man. "If it weren't for you, I think I would have gone crazy," says the man. "You and Father Duffy."

They talk and eat the meal the guard serves. The newsman makes no notes; he already knows more about the man than he can ever write. After the meal the men shake hands and the newsman leaves. The man returns to his Bible as the others along the corridor eat the extra ice cream he had ordered.

The day moves on. Then, at five o'clock, the telephone rings. A moment later a sharp knock announces a new arrival. It is the barber, a convict doing "two to five."

He speaks a cheery greeting to Death Row in general, then tests the barber chair, pumping it up and down and whirling it around while the guard calls to the occupant of Cell 3: "Guess you'd better get your hair cut now." His voice is matter-of-fact.

The cell door opens and the condemned man walks quickly to the chair, eyes straight ahead. He sits down and the barber adjusts the white apron around his neck and over his lap. The clippers hum and a white spot appears on the crown of the man's head.

The barber tilts his head and squints, purses his lips, while the clippers buzz again. Then he glances at the guard, who nods. The white patch of scalp is large enough.

Quickly the barber strokes lather from a cup and shaves the spot until it glistens. He cleanses the spot with a damp towel, brushes the hair back briskly until the island of white is all but obscured.

As the barber works, changes are taking place along the cell block. The guard transfers the condemned's meager belongings from Cell 3 to Cell 8, immediately adjacent to the shower stall and just three or four steps from the little green door. Another guard has entered Death Row with a neatly-wrapped bundle in his arms. As the man rises from the barber's chair, the guard walks the length of the corridor and places the bundle on the empty chair. The condemned man moves to his new cell door and stands examining a darkening patch of red sky beyond the high windows as it catches the final rays of the setting sun. Finally he enters the cell.

The night guard arrives. So does the food wagon. The condemned man had eaten his "last meal" in midafternoon. He will not eat this evening meal. The guard busies himself with handing trays through the cell door slots. It is nearly 7 p.m. when he reclaims the empty plates, checks the utensils to make certain all are returned. He places them on the food cart and rolls it to the door, where it will be taken away by a kitchen runner.

He walks down the corridor, nods to the figure standing there behind the bars. "Would you take your shower now?" he asks.

(They all die clean; and while the condemned is in the shower, the guard unwraps the bundle and places the contents on the man's cot. This, too, is an integral part of the ritual, for the condemned is to act as if he is unaware that the bundle is his death costume: blue serge Eisenhower battle jacket with slacks to match, khaki shirt, socks and soft slippers. He will wear this garb to his grave unless family or friends provide something else.)

By 8 p.m. the man is dressed. Familiar noises lap at his subconscious—subdued but intruding. He can hear the extra guards—needed for the night's work—chatting about vacation schedules posted on the prison lobby bulletin board. His eyes pore over the words in his Bible. But his cellmates are no longer to be denied the freedom they know the guards will grant this night.

"Thanks, friend, for the bowl of ice cream," one calls out.

The man smiles. "Think nothing of it," he says in a surprisingly loud tone. "You'd do the same for me."

"Yes, he would!" someone says with friendly sarcasm.

"Like hell he would!" another says.

Three taps on the wall of his cell draw the man's eyes to the front bars. A hand snakes around the wall and the man takes a piece of paper from it. It is a note. "Thanks for having known you, friend. Good luck." He places the note solemnly on his pillow.

He returns to his Bible. The telephone rings and all is quiet. It is a call to announce the impending arrival of Father Duffy. When the priest enters Death Row this time he is accompanied by two other chaplains. Father Duffy will spend his time with the condemned man. The other two will lend comfort to any who needs it on this upsetting night. This, too, is part of the ritual.

Father Duffy speaks softly with the man while the big clock on the wall ticks relentlessly and the large hand marches to the beat. The other chaplains are busy talking.

And then there is a loud *crunch,* a noise from outside Death Row—and all the chaplains raise their voices. But the noise swells into a whine, the whine to a snarl that overcomes their voices. It mounts higher, subsides, mounts, subsides, then fades away.

They all know what the sound means. Joe Byrd is testing his equipment, swirling the needle in the gauge above the switch to 1,800 volts, back to 500, up to 1,300, back to 500, hold, then a purring away to silence.

The telephone rings. Two new guards are admitted. Father Duffy rises and hands his chair to the night guard, who folds it and leans it against the wall by the coffee bar. The night guard then moves to the cell, key in hand. He is at the ready.

And again they wait under the harsh glare of the ceiling lights. They wait and listen.

A knock. The green door is pushed open slightly. The warden peeks in. "We're ready," he says.

Briskly the night guard inserts the key into the cell lock. He opens the door and the man steps out into the corridor.

"May I . . . ?" he asks. The guard nods, and the man walks back along the cell block.

"Goodbye, Joe," he says, reaching through cell bars to shake hands.

"It's been good to know you, man," says Joe.

(This is a sign the condemned is going down without faltering.)

As he steps to the next cell a long, black arm reaches out to clutch his hand, and a deep, husky voice filled with emotion blurts: "God be with you, man—and take care."

At that involuntary ending, the guards' eyes lock and then flicker accusingly to the black man. "My God, why did you say that?" their eyes ask.

But the condemned man smiles. "You take care, Tank," he says. "And God bless you."

Then the little tour is over; it lasted hardly ten seconds. He looks at the night guard, who nods to the first vacant space in the line—in front of Father Duffy, behind the lead guard. He steps between them.

At the lead guard's tap the green door opens instantly. The little troop files forward, disappearing one by one through the door and into the Death Chamber. The door closes and absolute silence reigns on Death Row.

The big clock says 12:02 a.m.

Assembled in the Death Chamber are those who joined the cast for the final act of the ritual.

The warden nods to the condemned man and steps back a few inches to make room. He glances briefly at the one-way window at his shoulder to alert the executioner standing so quietly beside his switchboard.

The prison physician, to the left of the chair, is nervously fiddling with his stethoscope.

The three guards place themselves at the back and on both sides of the chair. They wait.

To the condemned man three of the four men standing behind the black iron railing directly in front of the chair are strangers. They are the official witnesses, and the one he knows is the newsman who had talked with him, joked with him, offered him cigars—and had heard him out without comment as he tried to explain the events of the brutal and bloody day that had brought him here to this little room.

Now the warden's eyes recheck the scene, finding every person in the right place. He turns to the man, addresses him by his first name, asking in an almost kindly voice: "Do you have anything to say?"

The man sweeps the witnesses with his gaze. "I hold no malice against anyone," he says softly. "I'm not mad at anyone. I want to thank all of you people for being so kind to me. I want to thank my friends who tried to help me." It is as if by rote.

The warden nods. He speaks, and the words seem strangely derisive, but they are words wardens before him have spoken, and his voice is firm and polite. "Have a seat, please," he says.

The man moves to the chair and sits down. The guards move quickly, efficiently, to strap him in, to position electrodes on his head and left leg, first dampening the shaved spots with a saline solution to facilitate the smooth flow of the electric current.

The man is pale. His arms are lashed to arm rests, his legs to the chair legs, his body to the chair with a broad strap so taut that it straightens his spine to the chair back.

He smiles—but he tries to cringe away as a guard stuffs cotton in his nostrils to trap blood that might gush from ruptured veins in his brain.

A mask is placed across his face. The guard steps back quickly. The warden glances around once more; every man is in his place. He turns and nods in the direction of the one-way mirror behind which Joe Byrd is waiting.

The *crunch*. The mounting whine and snarl of the generator. The man's lips peel back, the throat strains for a last desperate cry, the body arches against the restraining straps as the generator whines and snarls again, the features purple, steam and smoke rise from the bald spots on head and leg while the sick-sweet smell of burned flesh permeates the little room.

The generator purrs to a halt.

The warden does not move. Neither do the guards. But the physician steps forward. He places his stethoscope against the steaming chest, listens intently. He turns to the warden.

"I pronounce this man dead," he says.

It is 12:08 a.m.

The ritual has ended.

Ventilator fans suck out the fouled air as the guards wait for the corpse to "cool off" before they remove it from the chair. They will place it on a stretcher now positioned on the floor. Outside the main gate an ambulance awaits to transport the body to a funeral home where friends have arranged for services. (If no one claims a body within 72 hours, it is shipped to Texas Medical Center in Houston for use in educating doctors.)

On Death Row the men are silent. The guard sips his coffee and reads the newspaper.

2

The Assignment

Huntsville is a small, quiet, unhurried community sitting on the red sandy hills of East Texas under a green umbrella of towering pines with a sprinkling of live oaks. It is an old town, rich in Texas and American history. Sam Houston, that tall Tennessean-turned-Texan whose startling victory over the Mexican forces at San Jacinto saved the fledgling Republic of Texas for its pioneers, lived, died and is buried here.

Huntsville was founded in 1830 by a far rover, Pleasant Gray, who "went west" from Huntsville, Alabama, to seek his fortune on the new frontier.

Today it has a population of 11,000. Mingling with the descendants of many of the state's oldest families are another 11,000 lively students of Sam Houston State University, famous on the sports pages across the country for its basketball team which, in 1973, hung up 25 victories without defeat to rank as the nation's No. 1 small-college team.

In the very heart of the city stands the vine covered walls of the Huntsville unit of the Texas Prison System. Some 1,700 inmates and prison personnel live behind those walls, but the city's life flows around the tall brick barrier as if the men, the cells, the workshops did not exist. There is nothing callous in this blindness. It simply evolved as an acceptance, a belief that the prison had been there always, that the unseen inmates would never be confronted as one meets neighbors on the city square.

The community and environs are served by the *Hunts-*

ville Item, founded in 1850 and surviving as the oldest continuously published weekly newspaper in the state. I am editor and publisher of the *Item*.

Like the citizens, the newspaper takes little notice of the prison unit. Only if some area citizen is convicted and incarcerated does the *Item* record it. Men who are sent to the unit from elsewhere in the state are the concern of news media and citizens in the communities where the men were convicted.

I have spent a majority of my years in Huntsville, but I was born in 1906 in the tiny town of Katy, then a few dusty miles from Houston. My father was a chemical engineer. I had no brothers but two sisters. I did a lot of hunting and fishing as a kid, but my father also maintained a truck farm and there was plenty of hoeing and picking to do. My most distasteful task was milking our cow. My father would tell me, "It'll make a man of you, Don."

We were Methodists, and I recall we always went to church earlier than the Baptists because our circuit-rider minister had places to preach after he left us. Sunday School, then, came after regular church services, and it made for a long morning's attendance for youngsters. I was baptized in a little white-frame church at an age too tender for the rite to have any significance.

This typical rural life came to an end when I was ten. My father was transferred to Illinois, and we settled in the Highland Park area on the North Shore of Lake Michigan above Chicago. Life was a bit different in Illinois; the pace was faster, we were more aware of the great city reaching up to us, and it was cold earlier in the Fall and later in the Summer. I never thawed out in Illinois.

My high school days were spent at the Deerfield-Shields Consolidated High School where, so the teachers said, I excelled in English and history. It wasn't until I had enrolled in the University of Chicago that I dipped my hands into printer's ink. I had planned, on the urging of a high school classmate, to study medicine, but I determined quite early in my college career that I had neither the temperament nor the inclination to be a doctor.

Chance took me into the campus offices of the *Daily Maroon,* the student newspaper. I watched wide-eyed the bustle of the editors and the reporters and eventually talked my way into this scene. At first I was a "flunky" running errands and such, but eventually I handled circulation and now and then turned in a bit of writing.

All the while I was working for a degree in Liberal Arts. A lifetime career in journalism had never entered my mind. But just before graduation I read a Chicago *Tribune* advertisement announcing a training program for beginners in the field. I applied and was accepted, at a salary of $12.50 a week. I had not yet turned 21.

My first assignment was in the classified advertising department, but soon I was shifted to display advertising. After a short stint there, the program director assigned me to the old Pekin Street precinct police station as a "cub" reporter —and the direction of my life was set.

The underworld became my beat. When a team of detectives roared away from the station in a bright yellow Cadillac, I would be bouncing around in the rear seat, holding on for dear life and praying I would still be alive to turn in a story on the murder victim we expected to find.

I stayed with the *"Trib"* for four years. Life was exciting during this bloody chapter of Chicago's history. Gangsterism was in its ascendancy under prohibition. Crime flourished and the names of Al Capone and Murray (the Camel) Humphry and "Big Jim" Colosimo and their minions made the headlines. It was a world of crashing machine guns, of clumps of bodies throughout "the Loop" and the near North and South sides of Chicagoland. Newspaper street sales were high.

But I missed the hot Texas sun on my back. My blood was just too thin for Chicago and those wintry blasts off Lake Michigan. An item in a newspaper trade journal alerted me to a job opening with the McAllen *Monitor*, a small daily newspaper down near the Rio Grande in the citrus and produce-growing "Valley" of Texas. It had to be warm in McAllen!

I applied for the job and got it—this was in 1932—at

$20 a week. True, the pace was slower, the news hardly as bombastic as that funneling through the Pekin Street Precinct station, but life along the Rio Grande was fascinating and I enjoyed my new job. I lasted three years reporting and selling advertising—before greater opportunity and more money took me to the Bay City *Tribune* on the shores of the Gulf of Mexico where I was paid $35 a week.

My days as a wandering newspaperman were brought to a halt through a chance meeting with the late Ross Woodall and his wife, Patsy, at a Texas Press Association meeting in Austin in 1937. We spent an evening discussing the newspaper profession and its changes and challenges. Mrs. Woodall said, "We wish we had a young fellow like you to help us upgrade our newspaper." The Woodalls were the publishers of the *Item,* and though I had heard of the ancient weekly, I knew little about Huntsville as a community. I was aware that it had a college and a state prison, and that the lumber industry flourished in the piney woods of the area.

But it also had the Woodalls, famous throughout Texas as leading members of their profession. I wanted to work for them and I let them know it. The *Item* was then a weekly newspaper (now thrice-weekly and planning to become a daily). I was hired and went to work that November of 1937 at $12.50 a week! The $12.50 represented a substantial cutback financially, but Mrs. Woodall had assured me: "Don, we can't pay you much right now, but I'll guarantee you won't go hungry."

It didn't take long to get settled in Huntsville. I moved into a small room in the old Peter's Hotel and Boarding House just off the Huntsville "square." It cost me $7.50 a week and this sum covered the cost of food as well as lodging. The old Peter's House was famous throughout Texas for its fine dining room and its Sunday buffets. Motorists from miles around packed their families into their Fords and Overlands and Essexes and chugged through the piney woods to Huntsville and the Peter's House for Sunday dinner. They came from as far away as Houston; that was 70 miles!

I soon found out that Huntsville news was just like that which any small town weekly newspaper thrives on. Misspell the name of the chairman of the local preservation society and the mailman will bring a letter complimenting you on your ability to capsule the exciting news of its last executive meeting ("The Huntsville Society for the Preservation of the old Tyler House on Pine Hill announced it was $37.60 closer to its goal through funds received from a huge garage sale. . ."). Then comes the knife—"I realize the misspelling of Executive Chairman Tulip Throgmorton's name was a mechanical error, but in case it wasn't, perhaps you might jot down the proper spelling on the sliding table leaf of your desk for future reference."

The mayor, the city councilmen, the manager of the Chamber of Commerce, the ministers, the principal of the high school, the postmaster, the banker, the football coach and the chief of police—they are the newsmakers and news sources in the small towns of the nation.

Soon I got to know them all in Huntsville—even the circuit district judge, whose appearance in town as announced in the *Item* caused a stir of anticipation in the populace and a few restless nights for the denizens of our county jail.

On my new job I learned how to operate a camera. I would cover a story, take the photographs, rush back to the office on press day, write the story, write the head, develop the pictures, lay out the page, go back to the press room and help put the page together, help carry the form to the press if necessary and then run the press if I had to run it to get the paper out. It was always thus on a weekly newspaper; ask the man who runs one.

My friendships began with the night clerk at the Peter's House, lapped out to include the waiters in the dining room, the men and women whose activities the paper covered, and broadened further with my involvement in the community and its people and affairs.

My political education on Huntsville and Walker County came, so to speak, at the knee of an old County Judge who not only knew everybody for miles around by their first names, but remembered the breed of their cattle and the brand names of their farm implements.

So I immersed myself in the life of my new community,

covered the city council meetings, photographed fires and traffic accidents and anniversary parades, attended luncheons of the Rotarians, the Lions, the Kiwanians and the Chamber of Commerce, reported on new construction projects and the passing of "old settlers" who had left their marks on the community.

I became so involved that my sporadic trips to the bright lights of Houston or Galveston left me as titillated as a country boy craning his neck under the gas lights to observe the gyrations of Little Egypt on the main platform of the traveling sideshow late on a Saturday night.

Life was good for the *Item*'s new man, trying out new page layouts, broadening news coverage, lending ideas to the advertising department. And my new friends were warm to me, always wanting to help in some way.

Then one evening when I was alone in the office, a call came in from Dallas. The caller identified himself as the manager of the Associated Press Bureau. He said Mr. Woodall had given him my name.

"What I want, Don, is for you to go over to the prison tonight and cover the execution of a man named Hemphill—Albert Lee Hemphill. All we need are the 'times.' You know, when he goes into the death chamber and when he's pronounced dead. We've already got the story written here. Call as soon as it's over."

He hung up before I could ask a single question or make a single comment. His voice had been crisp, businesslike.

I turned back to the typewriter, but my hands hung on the keys.

Execution!

Death chamber!

Jesus Christ!

I sat there looking at the half-written story in my typewriter. My mind was as numb as my fingers. The telephone on my desk rang but I could not find the strength of purpose to answer it. It rang on and on, and when it finally stopped the acid of reality began burning off the jelly in which my brain had been congealed.

The simple fact was that I had not known that men were electrocuted at the prison unit just a few blocks from my office. I had never heard any talk of such a thing. The Woodalls certainly had not mentioned it even in casual conversation.

But why me?

Suddenly I was angry. Mr. Woodall had given my name to the *AP* bureau manager. Why hadn't he told me to expect such a call? What the hell was going on?

I got up and went searching for Mr. Woodall. He was not in his office. He was not in the back shop. He was nowhere in the building. I went to my desk and called his home. No answer.

I leaned back in my chair—and as suddenly as my anger had come, a wave of shame swept over me. I was acting like a kid. What the hell, I had seen more violence and death in Chicago than most soldiers had seen on a battlefield. Gore and gunfire had been my beat. There the dead men became statistics. Murder piled on murder until they had blurred together in an overlapping montage.

And I was a reporter. I was expected to cover any assignment given me. I didn't like it. I still resented the manner in which I had been informed of the task. But I knew I was going to do the job.

I called the warden's office, told the clerk I was to cover the night's execution.

"Be at the warden's office at eleven o'clock," the clerk said.

He hung up the phone. Everybody was being damned brief with me, I thought.

I left the office and set out for the hotel. I spoke to no one on the trip, and I passed up my usual bantering conversation with the hotel clerk. I climbed the stairs to my room. I sat on the bed and stared out the window at the old courthouse tower down the way.

I was not much of a drinking man, but I would have gone for one had Huntsville not been the seat of a dry county. I sat on the bed for a good half hour, almost motionless, my mind and emotions swinging like a tavern sign in a stiff wind.

Finally I went down to the dining room and filled up on roast beef and creamed potatoes in the hope such food would settle me down. It didn't. I roved the hotel lobby, trying to walk down the heavy dinner. And then I ambushed the night clerk. He was an old-timer who loved to talk. There had been no executions for months before I arrived in Huntsville, he told me. He gave me a complete rundown on all the various units of the prison system, listed for me the names and positions of the ranking personnel, identified the executioner, regaled me with tales of escapes and escapes foiled. He acted as if I should rush to my task with a joyous heart.

I went back to my room but it had shrunk. Back to the lobby I went. I realized I had no copy paper, so I went to a writing desk for a sheet of stationery, all I would need to record the "times."

I noticed that my hand was shaking as I picked up the sheet of paper. In exasperation and anger I said aloud: "What the hell!"

Every traveling man in the lobby jerked to attention in his black leather chair. Heads swiveled, eyes sought the culprit. The clerk ducked under the desk extension and came skittering across the lobby. I apologized, took a chair and tried to be inconspicuous.

By 10:30 or so I had pulled myself together. I walked over to the desk to let the night clerk know I wasn't a complete nut. He gave me a close look and squeezed my arm. "Take it easy, old son," he said.

I headed through the lobby at a brisk clip, ducked out the door to the street with neck burning from the quizzical stares of the newspaper readers and, five minutes later, was trudging up the circular driveway to the prison gate. The vines rustled along the high walls and I could make out the shadow of the guard through the window of his tiny square outpost perched on the corner of the wall.

The gate guard checked my name with his list of official witnesses, pushed a button, and the inner gate slid silently open. I walked through to see a group of men to the right in what turned out to be the warden's outer office. They were there, I presumed, for the same purpose as I—we were the witnesses. We stood or sat in the anteroom, a restless group of five who stared at everything in sight except each other. At the paintings and pictures and plaques on the walls, at the desks that appeared to be clean-topped and ready for action, at the door to the warden's office.

The door opened with a suddenness that brought all of us to stiff attention. Out stepped a small, sandy-haired man who flashed a quick smile and identified himself as an assistant warden. He informed us we would enter the Death Chamber shortly before midnight, that we would stand behind a railing directly in front of the electric chair, remain silent from the time the condemned man entered the Death Chamber until the prison physician pronounced the man dead. Then we would leave as quickly and quietly as possible. He handled us with the assurance of a District Attorney who knew he had the defendant's alibi witness hidden away in a far-off state.

I reminded the assistant warden I was the Associated Press correspondent and would have to stay until I received the official times from the warden. He nodded agreement. It all sounded so official, and we settled down a bit. Some of us wandered out into the hall to peer through the darkened receiving and holdover pens and down into the long cell blocks, following the row of dimmed lights until they blended into a blurred streak in the distance. I wondered aloud if they dimmed when the executioner "threw the switch," and the assistant warden smiled .

"No," he said. "The Death House has its own set of generators. That only happens in the movies—the lights of the town going dim and the townspeople hiding under their blankets so they won't know, and all that tripe . . . ."

The wait stretched out intolerably. Then a door down past the holding cells swung open and the assistant warden said, "We're ready." He led us in single file through the door, through a series of gates and doors until we wound up in the darkness outside the Death House. My arms and shoulders seemed to tighten and I flexed my fingers for relief. The assistant warden knocked sharply and the door opened and we filed into the Death Chamber. The warden himself was waiting.

It was a small room, and when we were halted behind a black iron railing the electric chair was right there in front of us, hardly four feet away. I felt I could reach out and touch it. One large light globe hung in the center of the room below a white reflector, producing a harsh glare. To my right a dark curtain hung from a runner on the ceiling and I could see movement behind it. I surmised that it was caused by the executioner.

By now I was curious. I examined the witnesses' faces with sidelong glances. I noted a closed door to the left of me and wondered where it led. I constantly consulted my wrist watch, as did my companions behind the rail.

The warden turned and walked several steps to the door I had noticed, tapped on it sharply with his key ring and opened it slightly. The ear and eye of a guard appeared through the crack and the warden spoke just three words: "We are ready."

The door swung inward and open and a procession of men filed swiftly and almost soundlessly into the Death Chamber.

First was a guard. He stepped quickly to the left side of the chair. Then a tall, powerfully built Negro, followed by a priest, then two more guards. The door closed and the room was full of figures and shadows and standing before me was the condemned man. We faced each other, two strangers destined to brush each other in passing for only seconds. It was then I noticed he carried a white Bible in one huge hand.

"Albert," asked the warden gently, "do you have anything to say?"

Hemphill stared straight ahead and over our heads. He nodded his reply, then sank to his knees and sang "Just a Closer Walk With Thee" in a deep, rich and unfaltering baritone.

His head sank down and he appeared to be praying, his lips moving in the shadows of the light overhead. The iron rail creaked under pressure of clenched hands. We weren't ready for this; I know I wasn't.

At a touch of the chaplain's hand on his shoulder, Hemphill stood and the warden said those simple but terrible words: "Have a seat, please."

The rest was, I must confess, a blur. Hemphill either stepped or was propelled in front of the chair, and as he sat down the guards began fitting the electrodes to his head and left leg; the straps slapped chair and body as they were fitted with the speed of long practice across his body and around wrists and legs.

It was warm in the room by now. I could smell the odor of sweat. I hunched my shoulders and buttoned and unbuttoned my coat. Then one guard as a final act laid the Bible in the shackled man's lap. Both guards stepped back. One nodded slightly to the warden, who turned to the figure behind the curtain.

My pulse was racing and my blood pounded through my veins. My mouth opened to shout, "Get on with it!" when the warden gave his signal to the executioner. Then came the *crunch* I have heard so many times since.

The room exploded with the mounting whine of the generators. Hemphill's body slammed forward against the restraining leather straps, and the Bible came sliding down his lap to the floor.

I shrank back as the second jolt brought an odd red glow to Hemphill's skin and steam drifted from his head and chest. A dreadful odor of burning flesh enveloped us all. The prison physician stepped forward, put his stethoscope to Hemphill's chest. He turned to the warden and said, "I pronounce this man dead."

The ventilator motor came alive. I rubbed my face and turned to follow my fellow witnesses out of the room before I remembered why I was there. The warden told me that Hemphill had entered the Death Chamber at 12:01 a.m. and was pronounced dead at 12:07.

I hurried after my fellow witnesses. I almost loped into the warden's office, stumbling through gates and doors on the return trip. A minute later I was repeating the "times" to the night desk of the Dallas bureau of the Associated Press.

I left the prison quickly and walked the several blocks to the Peter's Hotel and Boarding House.

The lobby lay deserted and unfriendly, cold and rejective to the stranger I had become to myself and the familiar world around me. The night clerk said not a word; he hustled up a cup of coffee and I silently mounted the lobby stairs to my room.

The clammy dampness of an enveloping nausea crept over me as I undressed. Soon I was flat on my back on my bed, devouring air in deep, sucking droughts I hoped would steady a heart that thumped, then fluttered, then thumped again.

The room was intolerably warm. I got up and threw open the window. I sat on the straight-back chair and stared down at the pool of light circling the standard on the corner like an open fan.

The coffee was cold and bitter, and it made me gag. I dumped it into the sink.

I tried to read a day-old Houston *Chronicle*. The words blurred and became meaningless. I went back to bed. I dozed, and awoke.

There on the ceiling Albert Lee Hemphill knelt on the Death House floor as if on a movie screen, his face a chalky white. He opened his mouth and the sad blues of the old spiritual began running through my mind though not a sound issued from Hemphill's lips.

I closed my eyes tightly, telling myself harshly I was overreacting, I was a fool and worse.

I opened my eyes and Hemphill was gone.

But I was overwhelmed by the stench of his burning flesh. The bed clothes reeked of it. I got up and dressed. I fled the stinking room, but the odor accompanied me to the silent, early-morning square. I found a bench and lit a cigar. The flaming sulphur of the match almost made me retch.

And I lashed out at Albert Lee Hemphill in a wild rage that shook me: "You miserable bastard, you murdering, bloodthirsty bastard, they should have taken you out and shot your rotten head off when they caught you!"

I sat there, holding my face in my hands, berating Albert Lee Hemphill and every murdering creature on earth until I ran out of words and anger. I was totally exhausted.

I walked back to my room, undressed—and went to sleep.

3

The Functionary

A $5 check came in the mail for me from Bill Barnard, the Associated Press bureau manager in Dallas, for my coverage of the Hemphill execution. A note explained that my predecessor had been guilty of "coloring" the news, that I had performed satisfactorily, that from now on I was the AP "stringer" in Huntsville.

Since the *Item* was only a weekly at the time, it did not subscribe to the AP service. Had it done so, I would have covered the Hemphill execution as the representative of an AP wire service member, and would not have been entitled to extra remuneration. But a "stringer" got paid by the story when he was requested to cover one.

That $5 check looked as big as a billboard to a man making $12.50 a week and spending $7.50 for room and board. I kept in mind how much it improved my standard of living on the fewer and fewer occasions when the odor of Hemphill's burning flesh assailed my nostrils as I struck a match to light a cigar.

The irrational rage I had turned on the dead man on the city square faded from my memory. For one thing, I knew it had been irrational, but perhaps it was the only way I could have purged my mind and found the calm I needed for rest that grim morning. And the fact remained that Hemphill *had been* a murderer, *had been* sentenced to death and had died *according to the laws of the state*. The state, I knew, would not execute a man who did not deserve it. It had been my job to report the event, and I had done so. So be it.

It occured to me that the next time Barnard called me from Dallas to cover an execution I could very well do it simply by having the warden call me and give me the "times." But I remembered the line in Barnard's note: "Don't give us anything but the 'times' unless something unusual occurs." I would have to be on hand in the Death Chamber to quickly and accurately report on "something unusual."

And the day came when Barnard called. I accepted the assignment more calmly than I would have believed possible. The thought of the $5 check had much more to do with my attitude.

So did the knowledge that the man to die at midnight was a rapist who had murdered his victim.

But more important, I believe, was that my self-esteem was at stake. I was 31, in the pride of my manhood. I was a good newsman who wanted to be well-regarded by his peers. And many of my peers had covered executions as routine assignments, either at Huntsville or before 1924, when each county hanged its culprits at its own jail.

Thus armed, I witnessed the execution—and the next, and the next, and the next . . . .

Eighteen men were executed in that first year of my Death House coverage. Occasionally there was a double execution—one man following another to the chair. And once I watched three men die in a space of 15 minutes.

At this point you must be asking: *"How could this man have gone back time and time again to witness such an event? What kind of man is he, for Christ's sweet sake? Is he sick?"*

I have said I did it for money and my self-esteem at the beginning, and I suggest that in those depressed times $5 was enough to send other men on errands as strange. And to have expressed hesitation at mention of the assignment would have been a confession of weakness I was not prepared to make.

But there was more. As time passed I became in effect a functionary of the Ritual of Death. Prison officials quickly learned that I had a soothing effect on men who were ready to go down. It was not something I faked or practiced. I became genuinely interested in these condemned men, and they accepted me readily as a confidant. Candidly, I believe I had as much influence on a man getting ready to die as did the chaplains. So prison officials welcomed me into the official family, partly to make their job easier, and it flattered my ego. Prison officials don't like to see a man create a wild scene by fighting his way step by step to the chair; they thought I could help keep this from occurring. I was being used, granted, but it was with my knowledge and tacit consent.

Finally, I began to see my visits to Death Row as a form of duty because I felt I could help the inmates with my presence. And with that, I simply grew accustomed to the job. Accustomed, not calloused, for the time never came that I did not leave the Death Chamber shaken and to some degree haunted.

I had covered 52 executions when the U.S. Air Force decided I could help win World War II. My superiors apparently thought I was too old for combat, and I wound up serving 44 months in public relations and Air Force Intelligence. From 1942 to 1945, I saw nobody die, heard no sad Death Row tales. And the only out-of-the ordinary odor I smelled was airplane fuel. I was a staff sergeant and I enjoyed my life in the service.

One good reason was that I met my wife, Frances, during my G.I. travels. The brass had placed me in charge of a troop train loaded with embryonic tail gunners enroute to Ft. Myers, Florida, for training; on the return trip to my base at Wichita Falls, Texas, I was laden with notepads full of glowing reports on the prowess of men who had seen actual combat. From the notes I would write equally glowing press releases.

I changed trains in New Orleans, boarding another for the overnight run to Dallas and Wichita Falls. Almost immediately I spied a young woman reading a book while a young buck private tried to distract her and start a conversation. Since I outranked him, both in rank and age, I soon sent him on his way, which proved distracting enough for *me* to start a conversation.

She was Miss Frances Hawkes of North Andover, Massachusetts, educated in Italy and Vassar, ancestors on both sides registered passengers on the Mayflower, and living under the shadow (I didn't learn this in the first five minutes, of course) of an infamous ancestor who was executed by hanging for "lifting her skirt and exposing her ankles" as she tried to keep the hem from being muddied while crossing a street. One time, in a speech, I commented that my wife had an ancestor who was burned at the stake in old Salem and received a reproving letter informing me there were no burnings there, just hangings.

I also learned that the charming traveler was a fashion and promotion director for Rollins Mills, on her way to Dallas for a conference with the district sales manager. Her headquarters were in Des Moines, Iowa.

We took breakfast the next morning before arriving in Dallas. I was smitten. And by the time we reached Dallas we had established a rapport that appeared promising.

We parted in Dallas, but from Wichita Falls I conducted a courtship by mail, telephone, telegraph and any extra long leave I could lay on my colonel.

Then, one day, Frances called and informed me quite firmly that she was weary of our long-distance romance. She instructed me to find a place to spend a honeymoon; she was on her way to Texas.

Even a motel room was hard to come by in those days near an Air Force base, but my Captain saved the day. He was going away for several weeks, so he loaned us his off-base living quarters for our honeymoon. Then the new Mrs. Don Reid returned to Des Moines.

Shortly thereafter I received a telegram: "Find place to live. I am coming to join you permanently."

I found a place.

I had never discussed my coverage of executions with Frances during our courtship, and I didn't after we were married. I told her of my life in Huntsville, the pleasure I derived from doing my work for the *Item,* the friendships I had made. But I could never find the proper time, it seemed, to tell her of Death Row and the Death Chamber itself.

And there seemed to be no reason to tell her. I was away from Huntsville. In my small way I was engaged in a war that I felt, at times, would never end. And, it was reasonable to believe that the AP may have hired another man for the "stringer" job.

But that was not the case. My job at the *Item* was waiting for me after the war, as it should have been. And so were my Death House duties for the AP.

Soon I was back in the old routine—in the prison at midnight, standing with other witnesses behind the black iron railing, watching men die with the *crunch* of the generators, checking the "times" and telephoning them to Dallas.

Once Frances was told the purpose of my midnight visits to the prison, she never questioned me about them. And I never recounted to her what I witnessed. She quickly learned that I was accepted as a newsman for the *Item* in the town itself, that no one in the community apparently took cognizance of my other role for the AP. And she was a practical woman, I told myself, one who realized that in every job, every profession, we do some things we like to do and a few we don't like to do, but do them all because they are part of our work.

But one evening a friend was visiting us. Frances was in the kitchen preparing dinner. My friend and I sipped a drink and talked. Suddenly he asked, "Don, does covering executions present any problems in your marriage?"

Before I could answer, Frances came out of the kitchen. Without heat or embarrassment, she said, "I don't like to discuss the subject anymore than Don does. But I'll tell you, it distresses me every time because of what it does to him."

Neither my friend nor I asked what she meant, but she went on as if we had. "I know they're ordeals," she said, "because after each one he has a nightmare."

I hadn't known that she was aware of those terrible dreams I had learned to live with and accept. She turned back to the kitchen, saying over her shoulder to my friend,

"A lesser man than Don would have ulcers."

My friend immediately changed the subject. He talked on of his days in the military, but my mind was on Frances. She didn't know that I had changed my routine because of her. Before the war and our marriage I had left the prison as quickly as possible after an execution and hurried to my room at the Peter's Hotel. But now, after calling in the details to Dallas and leaving the prison, I would take off my coat and walk briskly against the morning breeze. And I would wave my coat in the air as I walked, hoping in this way to dispel the stench of burning flesh, which I was convinced had permeated my garments.

Sometimes as I walked and waved my coat I would laugh at myself, thinking how foolish I would look to a citizen who might come upon me.

But I didn't want to carry that odor into my home, where Frances and I lived in love and happiness—if any other person than myself could smell it . . . .

4

The Parade

Most men take up residence on Death Row protesting their innocence. All but a few eventually admit their guilt to me or to the chaplains whose duty it is to make their last days and hours tolerable. They admit guilt, but they claim mitigating circumstances, which they insist preclude death in the electric chair.

Life in prison? Yes.

Death in the chair? Don't deserve it!

After all, they know a life sentence in Texas usually means freedom in no more than ten years.

But there are otherwise intelligent men who absolutely refuse to believe they could possibly commit the heinous crimes for which they were convicted. Yearly, monthly, daily, hourly and unto the final split second before the bolt of chained lightning snuffs out their lives they deny. They shove reality back into the dark recesses of their minds, take refuge in the search for "new evidence," seek the magic of new and oftentimes dubious legal maneuvers, plead to the emotions of the public through unsuspecting (or cooperating) reporters. There are "last minute" appeals of the aging mother to the Parole Board or the governor, and the four-column picture of a careworn face at the top of the front page.

They deny and deny—never recant—even as the generators flex their muscles with warm-up whines, even as they plod through the "little green door" and "have a seat" and die.

This, they will concede, is "God's will."

Such a man was Jimmy Shaver.

He had been convicted of the brutal rape-slaying of a three-year-old tot in front of a San Antonio tavern.

Yet there stood the handsome, wholesome-appearing 32-year-old airman stating firmly through the bars of his Death Row cell: "I couldn't have done it! I just could not have done *that!*"

Shaver maintained his innocence for more than four years. Two separate trials (one on a change of venue) and other legal maneuvers had prolonged his residency until he himself had watched eight men pace off their "last mile."

"I was dead drunk. I was not capable of harming anybody, let alone a child," he would say time and time again.

Shaver and his lawyers kept the news wires clattering as they won five reprieves from state and federal courts. Each stay literally snatched Shaver from the outstretched arms of the electric chair. With each reprieve, his hope soared that eventually his sentence would be commuted to life in prison. His self-induced spellbinding and apparent complete faith in a new found Savior—he had become the complete bibliolater, poring over his Bible daily and hourly in his cell —turned hope into conviction.

The fifth and final reprieve—a dramatic bolt from the blue just nine hours before the switch was scheduled to slam him into eternity—handed Shaver his last 90 days of life. It came from a former cellmate in the Bexar (San Antonio) county jail who "confessed" that it was he, not Shaver, who raped and killed the little girl.

Now it was the day before his execution day and Shaver stood inside his cell door, his hazel eyes boring into mine as I told him the State Board of Pardons and Paroles had refused to commute his sentence. His stocky frame sagged a bit when I explained that the "confessor" had flunked a lie detector test, and that a woman had testified the man was with her in Oklahoma City the night the child was slain.

"I just can't understand this," Shaver finally replied, shaking his head. "I guess it's the will of God that I die. He's led me step-by-step."

He did admit to me he couldn't remember any Donald

Summers, the name of the "confessor."

Then he opened his Bible and read, looking up long enough to explain he was reading from the Book of St. Mark. "But I like Romans the best—Chapter 8, verses 34 through 39." He turned to Romans and read the verses aloud to me, and said, "Amen." These verses proclaim Jesus as the only personal Savior.

I asked Shaver if he could recall the events the night the child was criminally assaulted. He shook his head and replied, "I just can't recall a thing except I remember I was riding in the back seat of a car."

All along, I reminded Shaver, he had insisted he had not committed the crime. "How do you know you didn't when you say you can't remember anything?" I asked.

The answer came as if filtered up from the deepest recesses of his soul: "I just know in my heart that I couldn't, and I didn't."

He said he wasn't bitter. "I think it's better to die for something I didn't do than for something I did."

This statement deserved an explanation and I asked, "How come?"

"It's very simple, Don. I don't have blood on my hands and I can praise God for that."

Shaver apparently drew some strength from his grandmother, who visited him after my interview. She told him his impending execution was a "miscarriage of justice." The day guard later told me Shaver's eyes crinkled up in a smile at her words, and he reached through the bars and gently squeezed the old lady's arm.

Shortly thereafter, Shaver's father and an uncle visited him and gave him words of hope. The father told me he had mortgaged his farm to raise money for his son's continuing legal defense. He said he had hired another lawyer, a civil attorney. I shook my head, then loaned him enough money to send a telegram to his employer that he was returning home to work.

On the morning of his execution day, I interviewed Shaver's mother, an El Paso school teacher, in a downtown Huntsville coffee shop. She felt that Shaver was innocent, that another person had committed the crime. Unfalteringly, she declared: "I don't know why, and I have few facts to substantiate my claim, but my mother's intuition tells me my son did not do this terrible thing. I know in my heart that some day the truth will come out and the guilty person will be apprehended. Even if my son has to die, I still feel it is God's will."

She sensed that I wondered how she could remain so calm after the cruel hoax of the false confession, the journey to Huntsville for the execution. And she quickly made a statement the like of which I had never heard uttered by a close relative of a condemned man.

"I guess I would get more sympathy from the public if I wailed and moaned, but it's not my nature to be a hypocrite," she said. "I know, as does Jimmy, that death will be a victory. Tomorrow my first-born child will be in heaven."

I walked directly from the coffee shop to the prison for a final interview with Shaver. He was in a jovial mood when I asked him, "What do you know that's good, Jimmy?"

He laughed. "Nothing's good, Don—except the Word of God. That's always good." He opened his Bible and read aloud a passage from Corinthians which deals with death and the change from a mortal to an immortal soul.

Noticing his untouched breakfast tray, and recalling several of his fasting periods before his reprieves, I asked if he were fasting again.

"Yes, I began this morning. Not to seek special favors but to prove to God that I believe in Him."

He compared his fasting and praying to that of the Prophets. They had fasted and prayed for forgiveness of their sins. He said he had not ordered a "last meal." And he shook his head when I offered him a cigar.

Jimmy Shaver, the handsome, Bible-reading model prisoner who spent four years in one cell while mentally and emotionally outlasting five stays of execution on sheer denial of guilt and Romans, Chapter 8, verses 34 through 39, couldn't make it to the sixth reprieve.

He died on his 33rd birthday, his Eisenhower battle jacket barren of the Air Medal, Bronze Star and other decorations awarded him for shooting down six enemy aircraft as a tail gunner in World War II.

Head high, smiling, he went through the green door to a whispered comment from along Death Row:

"What a birthday party!"

And the wry addition from a neighboring cell: ". . . and with Roman candles."

I never told Shaver, but I had been convinced of his guilt beyond all doubt. Shoring up my feelings was a report from Air Force psychiatrists—and the Armed Forces always try to protect their own—who had used truth serum to learn several significant things about him. As an eight-year-old, he had watched his father beat a horse to death; this, the psychiatrists said, had a bearing on Shaver's mental outlook in later years. The report continued, further, that as a child Shaver had an aunt who would tantalize him, infuriate him, by tossing pebbles at him. The little girl, that night in front of the San Antonio tavern, had tossed rocks and pebbles at Shaver. The prognosis? If freed, Shaver just might commit the same crime again.

Henry Brown had pored over the scriptures, too, though his interpretation of them deviated a bit from the norm. It was this interpretation of "God's will" that put him on Death Row.

Brown already had served one five-year sentence for killing his first wife. He was to die for killing his second. He was sitting quietly in his cell, reading his Bible, when I tapped on a bar of his door to attract his attention.

"You look like a pretty fair Bible student," I offered for openers.

"Yassuh," he replied. Then he jumped right into the crux of the matter. "But I don't think it right for you folks to kill a black man for killing his wife."

This was the second time he had killed a wife, I reminded him.

"Well, it ain't rightly justice anyhow," he said.

I asked him how well he knew the Ten Commandments.

"I know about the Ten Commandments."

"Then you know the one that says, 'Thou Shalt Not Kill'?"

"Yassuh, I know about that one, too, and I still think you white folks are all wrong in doing this to me."

"Tell me why."

"I was married to two women. God gave me those women, and they both were no good. No good at all. It was my right to kill them. So I just got rid of them."

He didn't want to wear his battle jacket burial suit for the upcoming ceremony of death, and he told the warden—when asked for his last words—that when a woman's a no good thing, her husband had the God-given right to do her in. He squared his shoulders, compressed his lips and died, unrepentant, still convinced God was on his side.

William Henry Meyer, on the other hand, hadn't had much interest in the Good Book. And he knew nothing of psychiatry. He had just argued with his wife, Emma, for the 42 years of their married life, he said, and worked his farm near Granada, Texas. He was to die for killing his daughter.

I found the old man, a few days before his scheduled electrocution, sitting in his cell, apparently unconcerned about his fate. His bald pate flanked by shards of gray-white hair that shot up like devil's horns, his eyes blue and clear, he calmly surveyed the confines of his restricted domain.

He rose to his full and skinny height of six feet, three inches and reached through the bars to shake hands. His big, work-hardened hand had a strong grip for the 137 pounds distributed along his bony frame.

I offered him a cigar. Meyer smiled and shook his head, "I don't smoke. I live cheap here." He added seriously. "I always lived within my means. I never drank or gambled."

Meyer had not had a single visitor during the sixty days he had been on Death Row. Neither had he written to or received any letters from his family, which included his wife, four living daughters, three brothers, two sisters and ten grandchildren. He had received one letter from his attorney and several from ministers. He had not answered any of them.

But he talked freely to me about his family troubles. He said he and his wife, Emma, had been at odds for 42 of their 43 years of wedded life. What brought about the final argument, he said, was his wife's refusal to cook his breakfast one morning. They fussed. Emma stormed out of the house. She filed a petition for a divorce. In the petition, Meyer said, Emma claimed he had hit her with a rock.

"That made me mad," Meyer said, "because it was a lie. I went to my daughter's house where Emma was living at the time. I had my gun with me. When they wouldn't let me in, I just shot my way through two doors."

But Emma had retreated down a hall and into a third room. As the angry farmer fired at the door of this room, it was suddenly yanked open by the daughter. She received the bullet that took her life.

Meyer told me that later on his wife amended her divorce petition to claim he had hit her with a chair. This also was a lie, he said, but he did admit he had slapped her around on several occasions.

"She had a mean streak in her like her father," Meyer said. "Looking back on it, I should have killed her the first year we were married."

His cell was barren of decorative pictures or photographs of his family, though most condemned men prominently display family photos. He did have several small pamphlets on his tiny table and I asked what they were. He said he was a Lutheran, and a chaplain had left the literature. "I didn't want to make the man unhappy by throwing them away." He added, "I went to church regularly as a child, but after I got married, and the longer I stayed married, the harder it seemed to attend church because of the fussing with Emma."

I asked if his attorney was making any attempts to get his sentence commuted to life in prison.

"It really don't make any difference to me," Meyer said calmly. "I've lived long enough."

Would he like to see any of his family?

"It don't make any difference to me."

I commented on his appearance of good health. He smiled. "I eat well, I get along fine and I'm gaining weight every day—and that's the way I want it."

Meyer had seen one man walk his "last mile" during his sojourn on Death Row. He was Harry F. Butcher, Jr., a 29-year-old convicted rapist from Odessa, Texas. And the occupant of an adjoining cell was Lonnie Brinkley, a Houston murderer whose execution would follow that of Meyer's by two days. Brinkley and Meyer had spent time together in the Harris County jail while awaiting their trials and were well-acquainted when they arrived in Huntsville. Brinkley told me the old man had built a pretty good shell around himself and would "do fine when the time comes."

He seemed unreal to me, this unrepentant man, so indifferent to his fate. I doubt that his pulse jumped one beat as he walked along the corridor to the Death Chamber. I can still see his white hair spiking straight up from the sides of his bald head and glinting in the bright light of the Death Chamber.

He examined the chair and its dangling straps and the electrodes with a curious eye and turned when the warden spoke to him.

"Meyer, do you have . . ."

"No," came the stolid reply.

Meyer stepped to the front of the chair, sat down, and died.

Unafraid in life, Henry William Meyer lay unwanted in death. Nobody would claim his body. So I wrote a brief follow-up story about this odd man and the AP sent it out on its trunk wires. A letter arrived at the prison from a lady in Virginia. She had read the story about the "odd" man whose body nobody would claim. She wanted to send $50 to buy him a burial plot. She added: "Immortality is somebody remembering another." The warden notified her that Meyer's body had been forwarded to the Texas Medical Center in Houston.

William K. Jones refused to be interviewed before he marched resolutely to his execution, but he did write me a letter.

Jones was a Georgia-born railroader—blue-eyed, gray-haired and balding. A heavy-bodied man of 58, he weighed more than 200 pounds when he went down.

I had twice tried to get him to talk, to no avail, and was resigned to filing a few words on the "times."

Jones surprised me. He handed me a one-page statement handwritten on a sheet of lined notebook paper. In it he attempted to justify his actions in murdering wife and daughter in cold blood.

Jones titled his composition simply "My Last Statement."

He wrote: "If we could see our Mistakes before we make them it would save millions and millions of Heartaches, and would save a world full of trouble.

"I am sorry that I killed my dear Wife and Daughter. Just as sorry as I can be for I loved them with all my Heart.

"But God being my Witness and judge, I did not Kill them for any insurance money (an argument the prosecutor had rammed home with the jury). The reason and only reason I Killed them was that I was looseing my job with the Rail Road and I couldent see how I could Suport them any longer as well as they deserved and as well as I wanted to. I just couldent face them in the disgrace of being fired from my Job.

"It worried me so till I thought they would be better of dead and I thought I would rather they were dead than see them in such want and drudgery. So I Killed them. I have been teriblly Sorry that I did ever since, and I want to die now and go on to be with them.

"I believe it is my duty to die for killing them. I never could want to live any longer with out them. Please every body for give me. Dear Father in Heaven please for give me all my sins, and please accept me as one of thy children I pray, in Jesus Name I pray. Amen."

It was a frosty night, and I could see my breath in the air as I huddled in my topcoat and struck out for home in double time through the midnight darkness after watching Jones' punishment.

My story on Railroader Jones brought a few letters— they usually are addressed, "Don Reid, Huntsville, Texas" —mostly expressing sympathy for Jones, wondering if it had been absolutely necessary to fire him from his job. This wasn't the type of crime that captures headlines from coast to coast. There were just a few words in the state metropolitan newspapers to let the readers know the Press was aware of what was going on.

I also had wondered why Jones was fired, and I resolved to find out. But I got caught up in my work at the *Item* . . . and the chair was always ready for the next condemned man.

If Henry William Meyer was unwanted and rejected, the unswerving loyalty of two women tossed callously aside by J.B. Patterson and Jack Farmer almost made a shambles of the rigidly scheduled Ritual of Death.

Patterson was a six-footer so thin and scrawny his arms and legs were like broomsticks. Jug ears framed a skinny face from which green eyes peered out from beneath bushy, sandy brows. He was 44 and balding, a country bumpkin who had left his wife and eight children for a city siren—and had left the siren dead on a Houston supermarket floor when he learned she had betrayed him.

While Patterson was having his fling, his wife had divorced him and remarried. Patterson's case was so "open and shut" that he got not one stay of execution. But as he was sweating out his brief 60 days on Death Row, the ex-wife and her new husband wrote him letters of encouragement and tried to help him in other ways.

At 8 o'clock on the night Patterson was to be executed —three hours after visiting time and four hours until his "last mile" walk—my telephone rang. Warden Marcus Heath's voice rang in my ear. "Don! A terrible thing! Patterson's ex-wife and all eight of his kids are standing outside the gate and they're crying and begging to see him. It's a hell of thing!"

I said I'd be right over.

I hustled over to the prison, skirted the sobbing children on the front steps, and made my way to Death Row.

Patterson stood white-faced in his cell. The other condemned men, as unnerved as Patterson by now, were pacing their cells, caught up in this singular drama.

45

I huddled with the warden and the chaplain in front of Patterson's cell. He stood at the door and listened to us try to solve the problem. Finally he spoke.

"Write this down, Don," he said.

I got out my pad and pencil.

"Tell them to remember me the way it was on the farm when we'd all sit around the fire and pop corn and sing and I'd play my guitar. Tell them I love them all, but all I want is for them to remember the good times . . . ."

I scribbled down the words, then went with Warden Heath and the chaplain to the main office to put the statement in shape to be read. Then we went to the main gate and the steps.

It was cold, and the children looked like little robins in their multicolored coats and scarves. Their faces looked up at us expectantly, and the floodlights beaming on them revealed the rivulets of tears.

"When will we see our daddy?" one child asked through her sobs.

My heart broke for her. As gently as I could I told them that their father agreed with officials that they shouldn't visit him now. And I read the "letter" he had sent them.

It was magical. The sobbing stopped. The mother began drying their tears and I got out my handkerchief and helped her. When this was done, the woman looked at me and said, "Thank you, sir."

Then, herding the children ahead of her, she walked away into the darkness.

As for Patterson, he calmed down completely and went down with dignity, satisfied that he had done his best for his children.

Two years later the incident was almost duplicated in the case of Jack Farmer. He had been convicted of murdering his second wife when he learned she had been married four times previously, not once as he said she had told him.

He was an interesting man, half Irish, half Indian, with deep-set gray eyes twinkling in a ruddy face. This and a thatch of thick, dark hair gave him the look of the young Hemingway. He was a paint and paperhanger contractor, but he loved most of all to raise flowers and vegetables and this, he said, he missed most of all while on Death Row.

When I asked him about his crime he shook his head. "Nobody will ever understand the reason for what I did, Don, not even myself. I'm not making excuses, but I was drunk all that day."

On the day he was to die, his first wife, their eight children, his former mother-in-law and one grandchild were on their way to Huntsville from far West Texas. Car trouble on the road made them arrive at the prison after the 5 p.m. visiting deadline.

Again the condemned man was consulted, again the same decision was reached, again the warden, the chaplain and I talked to the group on the prison steps.

By the time Farmer died, his family was well along its 400-mile journey home.

As Farmer was strapped in the chair, he smiled and winked at the assembled witnesses. "Make a good fight of it, boys," he said. He was trying to say something else when the electric jolt hit him.

Fred Jones had a wry, gritty humor that appealed to me. He was a grocer from West Texas, father of three children.

From the reports on Jones I learned that he had summoned his assistant to his office one morning for a conference. The assistant was a handsome ex-marine, a war hero. Jones had congratulated him on his good work and had given him a raise in pay. While the happy assistant was expressing his gratitude, Jones accused him of romancing Mrs. Jones—and had promptly shot the assistant dead.

When I asked Jones about the report, his blue eyes smiled at me. "Why, Mr. Reid, the man was a good worker —and I think he was richly rewarded on both counts."

Despite the jury verdict, there was some sympathy and support for the condemned man in his community, and Jones' hopes soared for a commutation of sentence.

Even after his head was shaved, the better to fit the electrode, Jones told me with great conviction: "I'll never die in the chair, Don. You just wait and see. That telephone will ring from the warden's office. I know it!"

And Jones was right! He was walking through the green door, the electric chair squatting not three feet away, when the telephone on Death Row rang. Governor Allan Shivers had called the State Board of Pardons and Paroles, and the board had recommended a three-day stay to further study the case.

Three nights later the telephone refused to speak. Jones tossed it a reproachful glance, then walked to the chair and was executed.

The row of crosses marching across the month of April on the calendar on the wall told me it was Nearvel Moon's cell. I had just written a story on the success of the annual Azalea Trail through Huntsville's leading gardens and walked the several blocks of sun-washed streets to the prison to pick up a 300-word interview with the semi-illiterate white boy who, by now, had probably heard his death warrant read to him by the assistant warden.

Moon was to die that night for an absolutely senseless triple murder. He had happened upon the people accidentally as he wandered through the deserted Addicks Dam flood control area west of Houston. The trio—Bertran J. Appleton, his 11-year-old son Steven, and a family friend, Lee Hanson—were target practicing, and young Moon asked to borrow the rifle for a shot. He turned the gun on the three and shot them all to death. It was a shocking act that drew nation-wide attention.

As I reached his cell Moon cut loose with a blast at Harris County District Attorney Dan Walton (now a judge) and Walton's staff.

"He's not a district attorney, he's a big crook," Moon shouted, and the guard came over and stared at him. Moon calmed down.

He continued in a lower tone. "They just caught me first. I just happened along and those deputy sheriffs found themselves a patsy. They chained me to a tree for hours and I liked to froze to death until they finally unchained me and carried me to jail."

"Didn't you sign a confession?" I asked Moon.

"Sure I signed a confession. But I had my own reasons for signing it. They threatened to hurt my mother and my girlfriend if I didn't."

The curly-haired youth refused to say who "they" were. He stopped talking for a moment and brooded. Then his face brightened and he laughed out loud.

"They tell me I'm the youngest person ever to receive the death penalty from Harris County!" he exclaimed. He seemed to relish this bit of information.

Then he was off again with his explanation. "I told those deputies I had seen a man run across the creek near the dam. He was about five feet, eight inches tall and he wore a red shirt and dark trousers. But they wouldn't listen to me.

"After that I wasn't surprised at anything that happened. I sure wasn't surprised that they gave me the chair. I even told my lawyer that as long as I didn't have any money to buy the D.A. I was gonna burn." He shook his head. "And I'm gonna burn, and I'm as ready as I'll ever be. I've never been afraid of death, and I'll never be. But it doesn't make much difference how I feel about it. I knew from the first that I would burn. I hope they're satisfied."

Then, in a surprising turn, he spoke a word of forgiveness for those who had had prosecuted him. "I pray that those guys who sinned against me will be forgiven." I couldn't tell if he meant it.

Moon hated Houston newsmen and had refused to be interviewed by anyone but me. When his mind leaped ahead to the walk to the Death Chamber that night, he snarled, "If Saul Friedman comes to watch me burn, I'll kill him!" Friedman was a Houston *Chronicle* reporter at the time.

Nearvel Moon *was* ready that night. When the warden peeked through the partially open green door to the Death Chamber and said, "We're ready," Moon shrugged off the guards, left the chaplain in his wake, and tromped on the heels of the column leader right through the door. All the while, a toothpick waved jauntily from between his lips.

"Nearvel," asked the warden, "have you anything to say?"

Moon glanced about the execution chamber. His eyes probed the chair and its appurtenances, then fixed themselves on mine. He took the toothpick from his mouth and drilled me with his brown eyes.

"Yeah! I got something to say!" he shouted. "I'm innocent!"

He stepped quickly, almost arrogantly to the chair.

Shackled and wired and hooded for death, Moon beat the executioner to the switch with one final shout.

"I'm innocent. I'm inno . . ."

Crunch!

They plucked Moon's toothpick from his clenched fist when they laid out his corpse on the stretcher beside the chair.

Nearvel Moon was guilty, I believe, of the merciless blood bath. I had felt that Moon was protesting too much because he felt it was expected of him by his Death Row buddies. He had been a model and neighborly prisoner despite his surliness with outsiders.

He was 19 years old when he went down.

Nearvel Moon knew he was going to pay his dues to society and, apparently, wanted to get it over with as soon as possible.

Albert Edwards knew he was going to die, too, but he refused to let his arrogance and contempt for his oppressors stand in the way of a desire to live just a bit longer.

Edwards was a white man, an ex-warehouse worker and an ex-taxi driver. Behind those blue eyes staring from his habitually worried, bony face was an active brain; he and his attorneys had maneuvered several postponements of his execution for the murder of his wife and a man he had found in a car with her.

He walked to the Death Chamber with a cocky stride, puffing on a cigarette. And when the warden asked him if he had any last statement to make, Edwards turned toward me. I was just three feet away from him, behind the railing. His thin face flushed a brick red.

What followed was an unprintable, vicious, wandering

tirade against me, the press, the police, the legal profession. Anything and everything. On he ranted—on and on past ten minutes, twenty minutes, thirty minutes. The warden, guards, witnesses looked on and listened helplessly.

His cigarette had gone out and he waved the butt as a teacher's rule as he laid out point after point. Finally he paused in his torrent of general abuse to snarl at me: "Now, you smart-assed bastard, you don't have the guts to print this!"

Before he could catch his breath for another onslaught, I leaned over the railing and said: "Edwards, you've talked for half an hour or more without saying one thing of importance to your case. Now, if you have something to say worthwhile, I'll see that it gets printed."

Edwards hurled his cigarette butt to the floor, stomped on it (an odd gesture, under the circumstances), turned to the chair and sat down without another word.

He had entered the Death Chamber at 12:03 a.m., had spoken his "last word," and was pronounced dead by the prison physician at 12:42 a.m. Most executions, including those of the condemned who fight their way to the chair, take little more than six minutes.

The warden thanked me later; he hadn't known how to shut up Edwards without knocking him out. The man could have filibustered against death for hours until exhaustion felled him. I don't know why Edwards chose me as the victim of his tirade. Perhaps he was stalling for time until the telephone could ring just one more reprieve and another thirty days of hope that he eventually would escape his prison bars.

Death Row had resounded only to the musical notes of the inmates' radios until Robert Lee and Marvin Eugene Johnson checked in. They were hillbilly tunesmiths and soon they were humming and muttering snatches of the ballads they were concocting; the bemused guards would peer at them and fret that "lights out" would not arrive soon enough.

The two Johnsons—uncle Robert Lee and nephew Marvin Eugene—had received the death penalty for gunning down a rookie policeman as he attempted to curb them for running a traffic light in Dallas. A third Johnson in the car, Marvin Eugene's brother "J.W.," received a life sentence for his part in the incident. They all were Californians.

Uncle Robert Lee went down first. I interviewed him the morning of his execution day, and was received with a smile and a handshake. He was an affable 34-year-old man with dancing lights in his brown eyes. He owned a lengthy police record that included stealing a hog in his native Oklahoma.

He talked easily and amiably about his music, and presented me with an autographed copy of a song he had written, dedicated to his mother, just before "I got in all this trouble."

It was entitled "Dear Little Christian of My Dreams," and was structured around John 3:16. Under the title and copyright line was the legend: "Words and music composed by me on my birthday."

The lilt on Death Row was muted with Uncle Robert Lee's departure through the little green door, but his nephew struggled on for 28 more days, putting down lines and dots on pieces of paper and humming bars and snatches of words that seemed quite religious in nature.

I had a long talk with Marvin Eugene Johnson the day before he went to the chair. He appeared in a happier frame of mind than any condemned man I'd ever talked to. During the entire interview he was smiling and chewing gum and smoking cigarettes—all at the same time. I offered him a cigar and was glad when he refused it. He probably would have exploded, trying to smoke it, too.

Young Johnson's father came to Huntsville from California and hired an attorney in a last-gasp effort to spring Marvin Eugene from Death Row. The lawyer told him it was a little late to make an effective appeal, but he did go before the Board of Pardons and Paroles to point out several errors in the original trial.

He argued that the state did not have the right to execute two men (with a third getting life) for one crime when only one bullet was fired. The Parole Board was not impressed. The elder Johnson made arrangements with a Huntsville funeral home to ship his son's body back to California, then waited out the execution in a motel room.

Marvin Eugene, caught up in the swirls of another composition, scratched away at a sheet of paper on his execution day. He came through the green door chewing his gum furiously. Just before he died he winked at me as if to say, "I almost got that song down on paper!"

Incidentally, ten Johnsons have been executed in Texas since 1924—a name more common on Death Row than any other, Smith and Jones included. Of the ten, only the two hillbilly song writers were white. The other eight were black.

On occasion the condemned fast in the belief it will help wash away their sins. Jimmy Shaver did, you will recall. So did Flandell Fite, a 27-year-old Dallas Negro who insisted that by denying himself his daily sustenance he had achieved positive results.

"I am positive that I will be freed," he informed me.

He had only one good eye, and he held his face at a slight angle so he could keep me in full view.

"I have had a vision, and in it God told me that He stands between me and the electric chair."

Was he actually guilty of his part in the rape of a white girl? Another Negro was on the chair's waiting list, while a third was serving a life sentence for the crime.

"I won't tell you or anyone else whether I'm guilty or not," Fite declared in a ringing voice. "I'll make my plea to God only, because the truth shall set me free!"

Fite said he was fasting in remission of his sins. "And God showed me three folded bed sheets to reveal to me that I would be free. It is not over yet! Even if I get to the electric chair, I am going to strap myself in—if God lets it get that far.

"And even if I get to the chair . . . no, I don't think the chair will work. I have already made my plea to God and I told Him the truth. I am not afraid."

Around his neck he wore a crucifix, but Fite said he was not a Catholic. "I don't belong to any faith. I just believe in God."

But the chair did "work," at midnight of the next day.

Fite's fasting meant only that he sat down in the chair on an empty stomach.

Junior Lee Williams, too, was fasting on his last day. But not for the same reasons that gave Fite strength. The tensions that had been built up within Williams during a six-year fight against death had all but devoured him. The mere thought of food sent him reeling to the commode in his cell.

Williams was a sad-eyed 30-year-old Bay City, Texas, Negro convicted for an assault on a 15-year-old white girl.

He cocked his head toward the green door in making a point to inform me—right at the start of the interview that he was not guilty as charged. "I don't know what happened," he said. "I was with friends, drinking and gambling that night this was supposed to have happened. I don't know how all this trouble came about. All I can say is that I've been the fall guy."

"Any idea who did it?"

Williams shook his head. "All I know is that I'm not guilty. My trial was a joke."

I had found Williams propped up on an elbow on his cot, writing a letter.

"How do you feel?" I asked.

"Lousy! I just don't feel good at all. My stomach has gone bad." He pointed to his breakfast of fried eggs, pancakes, stewed prunes and toast. It was untouched.

He had resided on Death Row for three years, and his dark eyes, during this time, had followed fifteen men as they walked, or stumbled, or were "assisted" along that "last mile" and into the Death Chamber. In that time he said he had never eaten a full meal or enjoyed a morsel.

Williams had been sentenced to death twice for the rape, the first time in Bay City. But this trial verdict had been set aside by the Court of Criminal Appeals on grounds the Bay City court erred in not granting a motion for a change of venue. So Williams was tried again in nearby Wharton. The jury there returned the same verdict: death. Since then, Williams and his attorney had waged an intensive and complicated legal battle to get him off the hook.

He blamed his conviction on a previous two-year sentence from Matagorda County for forgery. He had served this term in fourteen months.

"They had to get somebody," he said. "They knew I was an ex-con, and they knew it sure wouldn't help me, so they blamed me for something I had had nothing to do with."

Then he climbed on the bandwagon which many condemned men seem to feel will ease their souls through the Pearly Gates—or at least get them to St. Peter's doorstep where they can plead their case anew. He said: "If my death is God's will, that's the way it will have to be. If I'm not ready by now, I should be. I should have been ready a long time ago."

Despite his bitterness, Williams read his Bible daily, and he said he felt good "spiritually."

How about that last meal?

"My stomach is too messed up."

Junior Lee Williams shambled to the chair hungry, his teeth clenched in pain from a growling, writhing gut, but with a fatalism that could come only, he felt, from "God's will." From a physical standpoint, Junior Lee Williams just might have welcomed death.

Nineteen-year-old Adrian Johnson, condemned to death as a participant in one of the nation's most shocking and bizarre crimes, certainly harbored no rebellious stomach on his execution day.

Johnson and six other young blacks were convicted in the slaying of a 12-year-old white boy. The boy was sexually molested and then stuffed into an abandoned icebox in a ramshackle and deserted old shack on the edge of Houston. There, in his dark and airless cubicle, the youngster died in terror and suffocation.

Yet here was Johnson eating heartily on his day of death. He had ordered medium-rare filet mignon, fried shrimp, hot buttered rolls, a cherry malted milk and fresh strawberry pie. He topped this all off with an order of whipped cream for his strawberries. He sat calmly in his cell, filling himself with a banquet fit for Howard Hughes. What was left when he got through was shared among the other men biding their times on Death Row.

Adrian Johnson was the only one of the seven to die in the chair. Another alleged participant, Joe Edward Smith, who was nineteen at the time of Johnson's execution, spent eleven years on Death Row, watched men don their battle jackets and march that "last mile." He received 22 stays of execution and then was granted a commutation of sentence to life in prison. He was on Death Row when Adrian Johnson went down, and he shared in Johnson's last meal.

Three other youths, juveniles at the time of the crime, were indicted when they became legal adults (in Texas, seventeen years) and were awaiting trial. Two others—still legally juveniles—were stashed away in a state reform school until they could grow old enough to be tried as adults.

Adrian Johnson carried on a bantering conversation with the guards as he trudged to the chair. He immediately dropped to the floor of the Death Chamber, kneeling beside the leather straps and protruding electrodes and made his last statement—"I pray that this will be the last time something like this will happen."

He then popped up to a standing position, handed a white New Testament to the prison chaplain, sat down in the chair. His eyes roamed among the witnesses until he found me.

"Take it easy, now, Don," he admonished me as the straps swished around his body.

Turning to one of the guards manipulating the leather straps, Johnson asked with the faintest tinge of humor in his voice: "Aren't you going to put a hood over my face?"

It was done immediately.

The young Negro maintained to the end that he was innocent. "I had no participation in this crime whatsoever, and those Houston police perjured themselves to send me here. But I've made my peace with God. If I don't get another stay, I will accept this as God's will."

It was by the will of the state that the first surge of electricity arched Johnson's body against the straps, stilling the last prayer already muffled by the carefully adjusted leather hood.

God's will? All but a few cry out for it, but generally they hope it is His will that someone in authority will pick up his pen and scratch out a life sentence for them—even as they take a deep breath and head down the corridor for the chair.

But not Richard W. McGee. He wasted little time imploring his maker for a miracle. He dreamed up his own detour around "that contraption at the end of the hall."

"No use interviewing him," the warden had told me. "He's a maniac. Has been ever since he got here."

McGee had, indeed, become a madman. He raved and ranted, day after day, night after night. His fellow lodgers on Death Row protested in vain to the management that McGee was giving them all a hard time. They were hollow-eyed from lack of sleep.

My first sight of him has lived in my memory. He lay stark naked on the cold concrete floor.

McGee looked up at me slyly, then shouted: "What do you want, slaves?"

My jaw dropped to my belt buckle and I recoiled a bit.

Then he leaped to his feet, picked up an untouched tray of food, and hurled it at Warden Marcus Heath, who had joined me at McGee's cell.

We ducked down the corridor and out of range as the crash brought McGee's exhausted Death Row companions to their cell doors to learn what was going on.

"Go, and sin no more!" shrieked McGee.

Then he cut loose with blood-curdling screams and yells, cursing us until Warden Heath and I fled Death Row.

A week or so later I received a message from McGee, relayed by the warden: I could interview him.

He was sitting calmly in his cell when I arrived. My muscles were flexed; I was ready to flee if he went wild again. I knew he had been sentenced to die for murdering his sweetheart's father, and in his madness he might try for me.

He was a well-built man with a thin, intelligent face. Now

his brown eyes twinkled behind his horn-rimmed glasses. I didn't relax.

He grinned. "How did you like that act I put on for the warden?" he asked.

I stared at him in disbelief.

He nodded. "It was an act, all right. All of it. I'm no more insane than you are."

I didn't say anything.

"You're wondering why I'm telling you this, right?"

I nodded.

"Because I don't want to go down as a nut. I want somebody like you to know better." He laughed. "I tried, my friend, but it didn't do any good."

He was wrong. The next day, I learned, he was removed from the Death House for a hearing where he was found insane and committed to a state institution.

Ten years later he was declared sane. His sentence was commuted to life imprisonment. Today he is a bookkeeper at a prison system unit just a few short miles through the piney woods from Death Row.

I haven't seen McGee since that Death Row talk, but I'll wager his eyes still twinkle every time he thinks about the days and nights when he "acted" for his life in a style even John Barrymore would have envied.

And so it went, year after year. Now there were no new "excuses" for the crimes—I had heard them all. I did not fault a man for trying to escape death, of course, and I believed that by listening to them I was, in some small way, helping them meet death with somewhat easier minds.

I had been covering Death Row for a decade. The number of executions a year had fallen off since those eighteen men went down that first year of 1938, but the chair always sat waiting and somewhere in the big state someone always was being prepared to confront it.

My attitude on capital punishment had changed little since the night I saw Albert Lee Hemphill die. When the subject came up in conversation, I pointed out that Death Row inmates had been condemned by an efficient judicial

58

system which had proved its merit over the past hundreds of years. It was presided over by competent judges who considered evidence presented by trained and experienced prosecutors, evidence gathered by law enforcement officers who oftentimes risked their lives in gathering it. That seemed to be enough for me.

By now I was the editor of the *Item*. I was absorbed in my job of helping it play its role of a good newspaper in a community of schools, churches and solid business institutions. I sometimes hoped, when I thought of it, that there would be no more executions for me to cover. Indeed, there were times when I could almost convince myself that perhaps my Death House coverage had no true value—and these times were growing more and more frequent.

And then, on a Spring morning in 1949, something happened that changed the direction of my life.

5

Buster Northern

The day began normally enough, but about ten in the morning a newspaper friend from Houston stopped in the office. He was on his way to Dallas; he wanted to warm up our friendship over a cup of coffee.

It was good to see him. He was a man I liked and respected, a top-notch reporter. We talked of many things, as friends will, and shortly before it was time for him to hit the road we talked a little state politics. He mentioned that the anti-capital punishment forces in the state would likely soon be flexing their muscles for another try at abolition of the death sentence. "Not that it will do them any good," he added.

I had little interest in discussing the subject, and was about to change it when he asked me a strange question. "The women, Don—do they shave their heads like they do the men before they execute them?"

The question surprised me. "The women . . . ?"

He chuckled. "You know damned well they don't execute women in this state, no matter what they do." He got to his feet. He was grave now. "No matter how foul their crimes, they don't get the death sentence." He shook his head and his tone lightened again and he smiled. "I don't want to sound unchivalrous, but it seems damned unfair that fifty percent of the population is automatically exempt from capital punishment." He was grave again. "And they commit about 25 percent of the murders in the state, year after year."

He reached over on my desk and picked up a cigar. He

sniffed it, put it in his pocket, winked at me, and went to the door. "I'll see you in a month or two," he said over his shoulder.

He hadn't startled me with new and important information with the first parts of his statement. I was aware, of course, that I had never witnessed the execution of a woman, and I knew from conversations with prison officials that no woman had ever ridden "Old Sparky." What *had* surprised me was his remark that women committed 25 percent of the murders in the state, year after year. I simply had never given such a statistic a thought.

But as I sat there in the office I knew the statistic must be true. I knew it because I read all of the state's major newspapers and many from out-of-state—and I read stories of women killing men and other women, and sometimes in the most diabolical manner.

My friend had said that women were "automatically exempt" from capital punishment, and in a sense this was so. If they committed the same crimes for which men died, then, in the well-ordered society I had accepted, they should die.

In quick thoughts I dismissed chivalry, motherworship and other nonessentials. Chivalry was only common decency once rid of its pretensions. Motherworship was a sickness at worst, and not an excuse for patent unfairness at best.

And so, for the first time, I was willing to acknowledge that the death sentence had not been handed down many times when it should have been handed down. If I could be electrocuted for a crime, then Frances, my wife and love, should be electrocuted if she were to commit the same crime.

While I wondered how many people in my state were aware that no woman had ever been executed, the telephone rang. It was Bill Barnard, calling me from the Associated Press office in Dallas. He was calling to remind me of an upcoming execution.

But it was more than that. "Don," he said, "I want expanded coverage on this guy Buster Northern. Some real 'in depth' stuff. Can you go over now and interview him for a story for the night wire?"

I said I could. And I asked, "What's so special about him?"

Barnard said a wealthy and prominent Dallas family was interested in the case. "They don't believe in capital punishment—they think it has failed. And they believe this Northern kid can be rehabilitated. They've told the Parole Board that if the sentence is commuted to life, they'll look after him in every way they can. The board is going to hear the plea formally tomorrow."

"I'll get right on it," I said.

Joe Byrd, the assistant warden and executioner at the time, went with me to Death Row and introduced me to Northern.

"You're a fine-looking boy," I told him. The words issued from my mouth without conscious thought.

He *was* fine-looking—erect, neat, fresh-faced. His brown hair was combed. He looked me straight in the eye when he shook my hand, something most Death Row inmates seldom do. Had I seen him walking on the streets of Huntsville I would have assumed he was a freshman or sophomore at the university.

"Northern," I told him, "I'm not here to hurt you, and you don't have to talk if you don't want to. I'll listen, and I'll be fair and honest with you. I won't color your story. But if you have anything you don't want printed, then don't say it to me."

He smiled, and that was enough. I got myself a chair and sat down in front of his cell. I studied his face for a moment, then asked bluntly: "Buster, just how in hell did you get yourself in such a mess as this?"

His reply was equally brief. "What would you like to know?"

I suggested he start from the beginning; I had plenty of listening time and he had several days before his number came up.

"First," Northern said, "I want you to know that I killed that old woman and I got it coming."

He told me he was with two other young men and a woman (his sister, an ex-convict herself) and they needed money. They had noticed the woman had a considerable amount of cash in her purse when she paid for her gasoline at a service station where they were also buying gas. They went after the cash, following the old lady, robbing her. When she resisted, said Northern, she was knocked down in the struggle.

"I stomped her to death," he said, simply.

"Why? In the name of God, why? Couldn't four young people handle an old lady without killing her?"

"I don't know why I did it, Mr. Reid. I just didn't care about people—anybody or anything. I was brought up that if you had fifteen cents, it was mine if I could take it. We learned to steal before we learned our names. That's all I was ever taught."

Northern realized just $12 as his share; at least that's all he had when he was snared by the law a few days after the slaying.

Then he told me a few things about his early life and his family. (Later in the day I checked out this information and learned he had told the truth.)

Northern's mother had died when he was four years old; he was the tenth of her eleven children. His father, who escaped from a Georgia prison farm and was never recaptured, had sired nine other children by a first wife.

Northern's particular world was populated by pickpockets, pimps, prostitutes, pistol carriers and killers. He had quit school after the third grade to run the streets. He had just started to learn to read and write.

During his teens he had developed a taste for marijuana, morphine and other drugs. "I started using them in the Kansas State prison," he said. He had served three years in Kansas, then escaped while serving as a "trusty." But, he quickly added, "I returned to the prison voluntarily." He had been arrested for the murder shortly after his release.

I could hardly believe his family history. Five brothers— Mike, Bill, Johnny, Tommy and Dan—had done time in Arkansas, Kansas or Oklahoma prisons. Four sisters— Bama, Marie, Marow and Bernice—had records showing prison sentences in Louisiana and Texas.

What had happened to the sixth brother, Jack?

"Well, the Army got Jack. If it hadn't, I'm sure he would have wound up in some prison somewhere like the rest of us."

He added that he knew nothing of his nine half-brothers and sisters. "I just hope they made out better than we did." I sat and stared at this boy, barely turned twenty, and sitting here on Death Row for stomping an old lady to death for twelve bucks.

Northern leaned forward on his cot and looked at me as if reading my thoughts. "I'm twenty years old now, and I think I finally know the difference between right and wrong," he said. "These people here, the chaplain, have helped me figure this out. And I've had lots of time to think about it, too. I killed that old woman and I'll take what I got to take. And I'm going to die as brave as I can. I want you to write that if you will, Mr. Reid."

The interview lasted two hours. After it was over I looked into the Department of Corrections files, studied the reports on Northern and his family. I learned a lot about the family's involvement in crime that Northern himself hadn't known.

I wrote the story in my office. It moved swiftly through my typewriter. I filed it by Western Union to the Dallas AP bureau, finished up my duties at the *Item* and went home.

Northern was on my mind. At dinner I began talking about him with Frances—something I had seldom if ever done before with other condemned men. She shook her head sadly. "I'm surprised he hadn't been shot long before this," she said. "No family life, no schooling, no religious training, no training in a skill or trade that would have helped him earn a living."

I nodded agreement.

"From what you say," she went on, "it seems he lived only to prey on other people."

"Yes, and I guess that shakes me up almost as much as his crime," I said. "That kind of waste of human life is a crime, too.

The next morning, a Tuesday, the day before Northern's execution was scheduled, I was just swinging into my routine at the *Item* when Barnard called again from Dallas. He was excited.

"Don, you rang the bell with that Northern story," he said. "The morning report from New York shows it got big play all around the world. News editors along the trunk lines want more coverage if we can supply it. Can you do it?"

I said I would try.

"Great! We haven't had such interest in a long time on this kind of story."

He told me the AP had given me a by-line on the story. He laughed. "You're gonna be famous, old buddy."

I hadn't planned another story until the execution, but I rearranged my schedule and, that afternoon, returned to Death Row. Northern was in excellent spirits. He was reading his Bible in the midst of the chatter and banter up and down the cell block. The radio was lending a musical background and the afternoon sun's rays were beginning to slant through the windows high on the wall.

Northern jumped up when I blew a puff of smoke from my cigar into his cell to attract his attention.

"Did Father Duffy tell you?" he asked, his eyes literally glowing.

Father Duffy was a long-time prison chaplain, and a popular man on Death Row even when there were no Catholics to be given spiritual aid in lasting out those final days and hours.

Father Duffy had told me, but I shook my head because I wanted Northern to get the lift from telling the story.

Father Duffy had entered Death Row early that morning. Northern had been waiting for him at his cell door, standing motionless in his white duck Death Row shirt and trousers. The priest had looked searchingly through the steel bars of the cell door and into the eyes of the condemned man, and Northern's eyes had never wavered.

"Do you accept Jesus as your Savior, with no reservations?" Father Duffy had asked.

Northern had nodded. "Yes, Father. Yes sir, I do."

Northern had gone to his knees, his head against the steel bars, and Father Duffy had reached through the bars and placed his hand on Northern's head. He had baptized Northern in the Catholic faith.

Now this young man of twenty was standing before me beaming with a joy I had seldom seen on any face—and certainly not on Death Row. Northern was taking the "Jesus Route" as many had before him. But there was something so absolutely genuine about his happiness in his conversion that it reached through the bars and touched me. It was not the euphoria I had seen in others, that dream-like hiding place where they could almost close the door on reality.

"You know," he said, "nobody ever talked with me about myself until I got into this big trouble." He looked around his cell and out into the corridor. He shook his head and grinned wryly. "That's pretty hard to imagine, isn't it— that a guy could learn something about himself in a place like this . . . and find people who really seemed to want to talk to him and listen to him."

I had to know more about his conversion. "It doesn't seem to me that a ninety-day crash course in religion would be enough for you to learn very much," I said, "and certainly not enough for you to have really been converted."

"Look, Mr. Reid. Father Duffy went out of his way to help me understand about Christ. He told me time and again that if I tried hard enough to understand and accepted God's word, that I would be saved. And I've done that. You have to believe me."

I nodded that I did, but after I left him doubt still tugged at my elbow. On my way out I passed some of the Dallas people who had been trying to help him. The Parole Board had turned down their plea. They were going to see Northern to help him over the rough time when they gave him the bad news.

But somehow I knew he would take it well, chiefly because he had not expected favorable action by the board.

I stopped at the warden's office to phone in a brief bulletin to the AP bureau that, pending an unexpected stay of execution, Buster Northern would die around midnight.

Then I dictated the night wire story Barnard wanted and I constructed it around Northern's conversion. I didn't let my doubt show through the lines. Later, after he was dead, I would phone in the "times."

I was late for the usual gathering in the warden's office that night. I looked at the other witnesses as if it were the first time it had occurred to me to wonder about them. Some, I was sure, were here only because of the fun they would have the next day telling the story of the execution around the sheriff's office or police station. Some policemen witnessed executions in which they had no special interest; that is, they had not participated in the condemned man's arrest or conviction.

But there was an officer from Dallas present, the one who had captured Northern and the others after the elderly woman's murder. He was a huge man—more than six feet tall and weighing over 250 pounds. I moved close to him and he acknowledged my presence with a curt nod.

"What do you think of this Northern kid?" I asked.

He looked at me with cold eyes. "I've been stumbling over the punk since he was born," he said. "He's no good. Never was any good. I came down here to watch him die." His cold eyes challenged me to dispute him.

I took refuge in turning away and greeting an assistant warden with more warmth and effusion than the occasion demanded. Then we followed him to the Death House.

Warden Emmett Moore was standing beside the curtain that hid the executioner, whose outlines we could distinguish through the fabric (this was before a one-way glass shield was put into service). The prison physician was standing to one side.

Warden Moore made one final check that all was in readiness. He tapped on the green door, opened it a fraction and we could hear him say, "We are ready now."

The door sprang open wide to the inside, and the small column of men filed quickly through—guard, priest, Northern, two more guards. Northern's split-to-the-knee left trouser leg flapped open and shut, open and shut, above his prison bedroom slippers as he stepped forward. The company came to a halt, Northern to the front but beside the electric chair. Northern's head was held high, and he smiled at the warden.

"Buster, do you have anything to say?" asked Warden Moore.

"Yes, sir," answered Northern. His eyes swept the Death Chamber with a slow turn of his head. "I hold no malice against anyone. I'm not mad at anyone. I want to thank all of you people here for being so kind to me while I've been down here. I want to thank my friends outside who tried to help me." He paused. "My last request is that I be allowed to say the Lord's Prayer."

Warden Moore nodded, and Northern sank to his knees. Father Duffy placed a hand on his shoulder. Then Northern said his last prayer. His voice was clear and never faltered. He had learned the prayer well.

He rose and turned his head to the warden as if seeking final instructions.

"Have a seat, please," said the warden.

Northern stepped to the front of the chair—directly in front of the huge policeman who was there to see him die. The man could have reached out and handcuffed Northern again.

Northern lowered himself into the high-backed oaken chair, then moved his eyes along the row of witnesses until they found mine. He smiled as the guards busied themselves. They strapped him in, positioning the electrodes after dampening his shaved head and left ankle with the saline solution. They straightened his spine, pinned it back against the chair with a quick jerk of the broad stomach belt.

"Goodbye, Don. May God bless you."

I felt the questioning side-glances of my fellow witnesses. I wondered at the reaction of Northern's huge captor.

"Goodbye, Buster," I said.

The last I saw of his face before the mask was fitted over it was the smile on his lips. Then the generator's *crunch* came and Buster Northern died.

As the ventilator fans began their cleansing rumble I

turned to apologize to the man behind me for my quick backward step just as the executioner threw the switch. My move was a reflex, holding over from an earlier execution when a leg strap broke with the first surge of power and the condemned man's leg flew up and almost struck my face. It had been a startling experience for me; occasionally thereafter, unless I happened to remember the incident, I reacted to that *crunch* with a backward step.

But the man behind me wasn't interested in an apology. He was heading for the door, even before the prison physician pronounced Northern officially dead. The Dallas policeman was nowhere in sight.

I turned my attention to Warden Moore and got the official times required by the Associated Press. Northern had entered the Death Chamber at 12:01; he had been pronounced dead by the prison physician at 12:05 a.m.

They were placing Northern's corpse on the stretcher when I left for the warden's office to dictate the story of his final minutes on earth.

 I stood in the warden's office for a moment after my call to Dallas. A strange depression had me gnawing my lower lip. It was a deep sadness, a feeling of great loss. Finally I shook myself, picked up my notes and headed out of the front gate for my car and home.

As I went down the steps into the free world I heard a different night noise. I paused to isolate it. It came from a dark figure sitting in the shadows, away from the glaring light. I took a few steps in that direction.

It was the Dallas policeman. His head was buried in his hands. Heavy sobs shook his body. I went to him and sat down on the low wall beside him. I put my hand on his shoulder. He looked at me for a moment as if he did not recognize me. Then he rose unsteadily to his feet. His eyes glistened with tears.

He shook his head slowly and said softly, "When that boy began to pray I wanted to reach out and put my arms around him and tell him that everything would be all right." And he began sobbing again.

I wanted to reach out and touch *him*, to comfort *him*, but I said something, mumbled something I cannot now recall. I couldn't help thinking that less than an hour ago he had told me it would be his pleasure to "see the punk burn."

He shook his massive head again. "I just couldn't bear to see him die."

"Neither could I," I said.

And it was *true*.

Frances was waiting up for me. She sensed my depression or saw it on my face. "Do you want to sit up and talk about it?" she asked.

I looked at that wonderful face so full of concern for me. I took her in my arms and held her to me. "No, Honey," I said against her warm cheek. "You go on to bed. I'll sit up a while."

She kissed me and left the room. I went to my study and sat down in my favorite chair. I lit a cigar. Suddenly an incident out of the past came to rest in my mind. An executioner, an uneducated but thoughtful man, had asked me, "Where does it say in the Bible that what we're doing is right?"

Glibly I had quoted from Exodus: "He that smiteth a man, so that he die, shall surely be put to death."

Now I squirmed in my chair at the smart-aleck casualness with which I had tossed off the answer. The man had wanted biblical assurance that he was doing the right thing, that capital punishment was condoned by God. Why hadn't I told him that I had searched the pages of the New Testament and found no sanction from the lips of Christ or His disciples? Was it because I hadn't wanted to upset him? Had it been sophistry?

My thoughts veered away to Buster Northern. I couldn't kiss him off as a punk kid, not now, when I knew in my heart I hadn't wanted him to die. I had wanted him to live, but had never said so to anyone. I had wanted him to live because I felt that he could have walked out of Death Row onto the streets of Huntsville and become as good a man as any I knew—and better than I.

All of the old arguments I had used and accepted since

the long ago night of Albert Lee Hemphill's execution simply would not suffice this night. My faith in the system had already been shaken by my newsman friend and his statement that half of the state's population automatically was exempt from capital punishment. Now I began to wonder if I had been mistaken all along about the efficacy of the death sentence.

I was adrift in an ocean of doubt and uncertainty. Why couldn't some one person or group or institution have helped Buster Northern along the way? Didn't anybody give a damn about what happened to kids like him? Why did he have to grow to manhood without the slightest sense of responsibility, without the slightest knowledge or understanding of the laws men are supposed to live by? The waste, the waste, the waste—the words ran through my tired brain like a refrain. The waste, the waste, the waste . . . .

Well, what about capital punishment?
The truth, Reid, what about capital punishment?
I don't know.

I was filled with shame.

I had been a reporter and editor for a full score of years. I had covered the Death House for ten. Counting Buster Northern, I had seen 94 men die in the electric chair.

And I didn't know a damned thing about the conveyer belt that brought them there.

As I sat there in my study, full of shame for the years of ignorance and neglect, there began growing within me a great resolve. At first I thought it was a counter my ego was building against the shame. But as it grew my burden of guilt slowly lifted, and I vowed that the resolve would not wither or perish.

6

The Voyage

The phone was ringing when I reached my office, and a stack of phone message slips was on my desk. I answered it. A radio news editor was calling from El Paso. He wanted more information than the wire service had provided on Buster Northern's execution—and he wanted me to tape an interview with the condemned man who would be the next to go down. I told him to read his morning paper and to call the warden to do the taping for him.

The messages—all marked "Call Collect"—were from all over the country. I sorted them out and returned the calls. Magazines wanted stories. Radio and television stations wanted taped interviews. "Get the innermost thoughts of the next guy who's gonna fry," said one news editor, "or get in the guts of all of 'em on Death Row."

One magazine editor wanted pictures of Buster Northern in his burial jacket and one of him cringing in the chair. Another wanted me to do a story on the theme "Are we turning killers and rapists loose on our streets to kill and rape again?"

I turned down all requests. The calls kept coming in for another day or so, however, and at such a rate it was hard for me to get about my work. As impatient as I was to get on with my voyage of discovery, my work had to be done —the luncheons, politics, school lunch problems and a campaign to get the state and county to straighten out a dangerous stretch of highway where, as one oldtimer put it, "We've been scraping 'em off that curve for years."

But I did not falter in my resolve to learn all I could about capital punishment. I decided first to "hit the books." I read almost every night. I sucked in information like a vacuum cleaner. I drained the local library dry and sent away to Houston for books I would find in bibliographies.

And I interviewed so-called authorities—those who favored capital punishment and those who deplored it. My bill at home sometimes ran so high that Frances would threaten to cut off my cigars.

I explored the files of the Department of Public Safety in Austin. Time and time again inside the prison I went through the filing case containing the records of who had been sent to Death Row.

I began going to Houston and other cities—when I could take the time—to sit in on murder trials. I studied the arrest records in the homicide offices of police departments and sheriffs' offices. I talked with cops and deputies, judges and jury foremen, witnesses and lawyers.

And I didn't neglect the greatest source of material— Death Row itself. At my hand was evidence not readily availible to the authorities I had consulted nor to the historians I had read. Not even the Federal Bureau of Investigation nor a Supreme Court justice had a vantage point so valuable.

Just as Northern's execution had pointed me in a new direction, so had his conversion forced me to examine my religious beliefs. No one has ever labled me an intellectual, and for good reason. But I knew I possessed a healthy brain and, I believed, an analytical one. So I began a study of religion along with my study of capital punishment. I was a member of a family of devout Methodists, and I had been baptized in that church in my early years. The code of conduct my parents had laid out for me had stuck with me through the years . . . and I had tried to obey the ancient injunctions in the scriptures. Had anyone asked me if I were a Christian, I would have answered quickly and positively in the affirmative. But was I? I didn't know.

On Death Row I found myself listening with a keener ear to the inmate's versions of the events that had brought them there. No longer did I automatically assume they were lying when they said their confessions had extracted from them by force. My studies and investigations had shown me that forced confessions were not as rare as authorities would have the citizenry believe. And I could not help but think back on some of those men whose stories I had so easily dismissed . . . and could no longer check to their advantage.

I was conservative by nature—and a political conservative. It did not come easily to me to look upon the status quo with grave suspicion. And during the long months of study and investigation there were agonizing moments as step by step suspicions crystallized into certainities until at last I was willing to accept that the system which sent men to their deaths was shot through with error, brutality and rank injustice.

Morris Addison was a tall, rangy Negro with sad mulberry eyes. I approached his cell with guilt riding on my shoulders. It was after nine o'clock in the morning; he was slated to die in fifteen hours, and only an hour before had I examined his records. He had been charged in the slaying of an Austin, Texas, used car lot operator, and I had been surprised—and alerted—at the speed with which he had been tried, convicted and sentenced to death.

He was standing at his cell door when I reached Death Row. He swallowed heavily when I stood before him, then blurted: "I don't want to talk to you. You can't do nothing for me."

"You never can tell," I said mildly. "Why don't we talk about it and find out for sure."

"Talking won't do me no good. Nothing will."

"Let's see," I pressed.

Addison held up his left arm and rubbed it with his right forefinger. "You see the color of that skin?"

I nodded. "Does that have anything to do with why you're here?"

The words burst out of him. "It's got everything to do with it!" And without realizing what he was doing, I think, Addison poured out his story.

Addison had gone to an auction at the used car lot, he

said, and had made the winning bid on an auto. His bid was not a high one—not high enough to satisfy the lot operator. When Addison went to pay for the car and drive it away, the lot operator refused to accept the money, Addison said.

"When I told him that everything had been legal, and that he was supposed to take my money and give me the car, he started cursing me," Addison said. "He called me a black son of a bitch, and you could hear him hollering at me and telling me I wasn't going to get the car. He started shoving at me, to get me off the lot, and said he was going to kill me if I didn't leave. He backed me up against a car, and I could see he was really going to try to hurt me, so I got out my pocket knife and cut him off of me. That's what happened."

The white man died a few days after the incident.

"Did anyone see all this happen?" I asked.

"They couldn't have helped it, but didn't nobody come to court to talk for me."

"Who was your lawyer? Didn't he try to get some witnesses in court?"

Addison smiled faintly. "My cousin was my lawyer. I didn't have no money to hire one."

"What about the NAACP? Did you ask for their help?"

"They didn't want nothing to do with me," Addison said.

I looked at my watch. It was nine-thirty. I turned away from Addison abruptly and hurried to the warden's office. I put in a call for A.C. Turner, chairman of the Board of Pardons and Paroles in Austin. He answered right away.

"I've just talked with Morris Addison," I told Turner. "Have you got his case on your desk?" I knew he would have it there; it is routine on an execution day.

"You know I have, Don. Why?"

"Did he have any criminal record?"

"Yes, a pretty bad one."

"Did the NAACP get involved in the case?"

"Some people from there came to see us," Turner said. "They read the police reports and other stuff and then said they weren't going to help him. Why the questions?"

I told Turner what Addison had told me. "It seems to me Addison possibly could be getting a raw deal. Could you find out?"

Turner didn't hesitate. "We'll put some investigators on it right now. Hang up and let me get to work."

I went back to Death Row and told Addison what had transpired. Then I did a foolish thing, a cruel thing. "If I come back here later and tell you that you won't have to walk through that green door tonight, what will you do?"

Addison leaped to his feet from his cot. "Man, I'll jump for joy! I mean it!"

His eyes were alive with hope—and I suddenly was sick at heart because my words had created that hope . . . and the odds were all against it.

I spent a restless day at the office. I couldn't complete a single project. I kept waiting for word from Austin.

And at three o'clock, the warden called me. "Don, Addison's story checked out! His sentence has been commuted to life! I've got Turner's message in my hand!"

"Let me take it to him, please. Will you do that?"

The warden laughed. "Yes, I will, Lone Ranger. Get on your horse and gallop over."

I galloped over. I got the TWX message and hurried to Death Row. I thrust the paper through the bars in front of Addison's face. He kept his eyes on me, never looking at the message, and in those eyes was such a dumb, animal pleading that I felt tears come in my own. "Read it," I said. His eyes dropped, and he read the short message. He drew in a deep breath, exhaled, then slumped to his cot. "Lordy me," he said softly.

"No jump for joy, Morris?" I asked.

He grinned. "I ain't got the strength." His face grew solemn. "I just want to tell you that I'll never . . . ."

I shook my head to silence him, and I moved away from his cell and out of Death Row.

Addison served a minimum sentence. He has a good job in a city other than Austin. I know because I get word from him every February 8, the anniversary of the date that was circled on his cell calendar.

Among the so-called authorities I consulted was a

Houston newspaperman. We were staunch friends, but I considered him a genuine expert on crime and punishment because he had been an outstanding police reporter and criminal courts reporter—and in these jobs he had demonstrated a sensitivity and grasp of human conduct not often seen.

I still have an article he wrote about Percy Foreman, the renowned Houston lawyer, and several paragraphs of it, I believe, sum up succinctly a basic inequity of the system. It impressed me deeply at the time it was written because my research had confirmed the facts in the article a dozen times over. Here is the article, in part:

> *Attorney Percy Foreman has defended in open court more than 200 persons charged with murder.*
>
> *Only one has been executed.*
>
> *This record speaks highly of Foreman's ability as a criminal lawyer, but it also raises a question in the public conscience, a question of monumental importance.*
>
> *That question is this: "Was the one who died more guilty than the 199 who lived?"*
>
> *The heart cries out for proof that he was guiltier; the mind must be solaced with belief that the 199 deserved to live because of some virtue they possessed that was not his.*
>
> *But the very preponderance of 199 to 1 denies the heart, the proof, the mind, the tiny fragment of belief. We have to accept that among the 199 there must have been at least one whose crime was as cruel, as brutal, as vicious as the crime of the one who died.*
>
> *Well, then, why did he die?*
>
> *Or, to turn the coin, why did those whose guilt was as great as his live on?*
>
> *A simple explanation would be that Foreman did not defend as well the one who died, or that the quality of the prosecution was higher in that particular case.*

It is true that during trial Foreman was having troubles of his own. His wife was divorcing him. He said he was ill, and there was a one-day recess in the trial after proceedings had begun. There was talk around the courthouse that he was shamming, and many felt that the jury believed this.

The state was represented by a brilliant lawyer, Spurgeon Bell, who had been hired as a special prosecutor. Those who watched trial remember that Bell, now a respected judge, matched Foreman maneuver for maneuver, yes, trick for trick, and in the end prevailed.

If we accept this simple explanation—that a man's very life depended upon the opposing skills of his defender and his prosecutor—then in all truth we must accept it with horror, with shame, and with regret.

Foreman, himself, feels that his physical and mental condition at the time was responsible for that death penalty. And behind his bluff facade he suffers for it.

Foreman does not believe in capital punishment. As a lawyer in business he is aware that many persons charged with murder seek his counsel in the hope of escaping the electric chair.

As a human being he despises the death sentence because he believes that it sometimes is imposed for reasons having nothing to do with the law and the evidence, that a man might live because of a juror's whim or die because of a witness' malice.

And the 200 clients have convinced him that the last one was not deterred from murder by the fear of capital punishment any more than was the first.

How many of the 199 would have gone to the chair if Foreman had not been their lawyer cannot be judged, of course. He may not be the best criminal lawyer in this area, as some contend he is, but it is certain there are worse lawyers than Foreman—and these lawyers defend clients charged with murder.

> *Do these lawyers' clients sometimes go to the electric chair because the attorneys were less clever, less persuasive than Foreman or his equals would have been?*
>
> *The answer—as any reporter, lawyer or judge can tell you—is yes.*
>
> *Further, many prisoners cannot afford a lawyer at all. In such cases in Texas, the judge appoints a defense attorney.*
>
> *And to the discredit of the judiciary and the Bar Association's shame, the court-appointed lawyer has been, on occasions, a bumbling fool with little talent and no enthusiasm . . . .*

"A bumbling fool with little talent and no enthusiasm . . . ." How apt that phrase. In my long months of research I had seen such characters in action, and one in particular I shall never forget. He was one of those courthouse hangers-on who lived a hand-to-mouth existence as a court-appointed lawyer, haunting the corridors and waiting for a judge to send for him.

In the case in point, he quickly pleaded his young defendant guilty of murder, then retired to the men's room while the prosecutor put on a *prima facie* case for a yawning judge and a bored jury. No state witness was asked a single question in the prisoner's behalf. The farce was over in a matter of minutes, and the defendant was on his way to Death Row. I doubt that the attorney could recall the defendant's name two days after the trial.

While investigating another case I came in contact with one of the most remarkable men I have ever met. The case began for me one morning when I stopped by Death Row to talk to a man who was scheduled to die within the week. I will not use his true name here for reasons which will be obvious later. He was 29, a skilled worker, convicted of beating to death a prostitute during a night of drinking and arguing in the waterfront section of Houston.

Horgan (I'll call him that) waited me out as I introduced myself, then blurted, "I was there, all right. I was drinking.

But I know I didn't kill that woman!"

How many times had I heard words such as those. He must have read the weary doubt on my face. "You don't understand," he said with great force. "Why don't you listen to me? Nobody's listened to me from the first. Nobody. All anybody's wanted me to do is plead guilty or die. Well, I didn't kill her. I wrote the foreman of the jury and told him that . . ."

I interrupted. "What did he say?"

"I haven't heard from him," Horgan said, and he slumped away from the cell door as if he had run out of strength.

"What's his name?" I asked.

"Walker. H.E. Walker. He lives in Houston on Quenby street." And he would talk no more.

I drove to Houston that evening and located Walker. He was an accountant for a major oil company and a deacon in a Baptist church. He had been upset by Horgan's letter— and something even more upsetting had occurred a few days after he received it. The dead woman's brother had come to see him with information that appeared to invalidate the crucial testimony against Horgan. Walker had gone with the brother to examine the layout of the rooming house where the death occurred. He had left there convinced that something was terribly wrong. And he wanted to see Horgan.

That evening I learned that Horgan's two court-appointed lawyers had made a "tradeout deal" with the court and district attorney—Horgan was to plead guilty and the court would give him a twenty-year sentence. But the attorneys had not consulted Horgan. When he went into court from his jail cell he refused to go along with the deal. He told the judge, "I didn't kill that woman and I'm not going to say I did."

The judge, Langston King, recovered from his surprise and ordered the case to trial. The jury was picked, the evidence presented and the death sentence given Horgan all on that very same day. Walker was the eleventh juror selected and he was made foreman.

According to trial testimony, several men and the woman had been drinking in the landlord's quarters in the waterfront rooming house. Horgan was one of the men. So was the landlord. The prostitute was Horgan's woman and he was angry because she had been off with one of the other men. He slapped her around some, and even kicked her, "but not hard," one of the drinkers said.

The other drinkers left Horgan and the woman to their arguing. Later, the landlord said, he looked through a door and saw Horgan standing over the woman as if ready to kick her. At that point, he said, Horgan picked up the woman and put her on the landlord's bed. The landlord protested, and Horgan, the landlord said, dragged the woman from the bed, picked her up from the floor and put her on a studio couch. Then Horgan got a pillow and blanket and lay down on the floor and went to sleep.

Horgan left the rooming house early the next morning, the landlord said. He checked on the woman, he said, and her breathing was "labored." He called police. The woman was dead when they arrived. Horgan was arrested when he returned to the rooming house shortly thereafter.

Horgan had no defense witnesses. The other drinkers had little to say. But the woman's brother had been sitting in the courtroom during the brief trial. And he had come to Walker, the Baptist deacon, the accountant who also owned a law degree, with a gnawing worry. "That door," he said. "The door the witness said he looked through and saw Horgan and my sister. I've been in that place. There's no such door where he said it was."

Walker had called the prosecuting attorney, and he accompanied them to the rooming house. They couldn't find the door the witness had described. The prosecutor was surprised but unmoved in his belief in Horgan's guilt.

This was why Walker was so excited when I talked with him. He felt he had to see Horgan. The next day he drove to Huntsville and went to Death Row. Horgan didn't recognize him. Walker handed Horgan the letter the condemned man had written. Horgan had a difficult time extracting the letter from the envelope; his left hand was shaking, but his right hand and the rest of his body was as steady as a rock.

"What's the matter with your hand?" Walker asked.

"Don't you know?" Horgan said—and he reached his right hand across his body and lifted the left arm. He tossed the left arm backward across his neck and shoulders like a limp banana stalk. Then he let it go and the arm dropped like a stone and dangled there. It was useless.

Horgan said he had been in an accident before the murder charge was filed. His arm was shattered, the knob on the elbow completely gone.

Walker rushed back to Houston. He called several jurors, then called Judge King. He told the judge about the door he couldn't find, about Horgan's arm, and he added, "That man couldn't pick up a child in his arms and put it on a bed, much less pick up a woman from the floor and put her on a bed . . . or pick her up in his arms and put her on a couch."

Judge King said he would look into the matter. Three days before Horgan was to die he called the parole board and recommended Horgan's sentence be commuted to life imprisonment. The prosecuting attorney wouldn't go that far. He wrote the board that he would "neither oppose nor recommend" commutation. The board followed Judge King's recommendation and Horgan escaped the electric chair.

But that was not enough for Walker. He believed that Horgan was innocent. He began a long fight for Horgan's release. He bombarded the parole board with letters, visited the parole board offices in Austin, visited Horgan in prison to keep up the prisoner's morale.

And he gained an ally—a woman who loved Horgan. She had met Horgan while he was in the hospital being treated for his wrecked arm. One of her three children, a son, also had a shattered arm, and he was in the hospital room with Horgan. She was a divorcee who had to work to support her family and herself. She lost hours of work each time she visited the boy in the hospital during the day.

Horgan told her he would watch after the young boy, see that he ate his meals and deported himself properly. "You can visit him at night," he said.

It was a long convalescence for both Horgan and the boy. Horgan and the woman fell in love. They talked of marriage, but she finally shook her head; she didn't want to saddle Horgan with three young children when both of them were near-broke from doctor and hospital bills. They parted, and Horgan began drinking heavily although he was able to work at his trade even with the damaged arm. He got into scrapes with police, and then came the murder charge and the death sentence.

The woman felt guilty. Horgan would not have been at loose ends and drifting if they had been married, she told Walker. She became Walker's assistant, in effect running down every piece of evidence in Horgan's favor that Walker's trained legal mind could conceive.

And finally Horgan was released. His arm had been patched up in prison. Walker got him a job, one he still has. He and the woman who loved him were married. They are respected in their community. And they still have a great, true friend, H.E. Walker.

Maladministration of justice, then, is no stranger in the courtroom, but my investigations showed it oftentimes begins in the police stations and sheriffs' offices. Police were not interested in Morris Addison's version of why and under what circumstances he knifed the used car dealer, for example. Addison had a police record and he was black; the car dealer was white. Addison had committed a capital crime and that was enough.

But lack of interest is no more rare than too much interest. Some law enforcement officers have deliberately framed innocent men, as all who read the newspapers well know. But many more, who would not commit such an outrage, will bend the facts to suit them if they are convinced a man in custody is truly guilty. They feel they have the right because their work is hard and dangerous. That they sometimes err is unforgivable.

In Texas of the 1940s, 1950s and the early 1960s lawmen "made" many of their cases on the basis of confessions by suspects. In some trials the confession was the most substantial evidence of the accused man's guilt. Judges were quick to admit confessions into evidence, even when the defendants insisted they were made to confess, and juries appeared to rely heavily on confessions in making judgments.

Perhaps a score of lawmen around the state made enviable reputations as manhunters for their ability to solve major crimes and their persuasive power in obtaining confessions. Two of them were close at home, and I single them out for that reason only. One of them is dead, the other in well-deserved retirement. These men were Sheriff Buster Kern of Harris County (Houston) and his sidekick, Texas Ranger John Klevenhagen. As a Ranger, Klevenhagen was empowered to aid any lawman in his area, but he worked most often with Sheriff Kern. Admiring newsmen called them "The Gold Dust Twins." Kern used his fame to build a formidable political following. The men gave the impression of bloodhounds straining at the leash, waiting for a sensational murder to be committed. Citizens felt that Kern in particular could not rest until every crime of violence in his bailiwick was solved . . . and they properly respected him for it.

After one headline murder, Kern detailed for newsmen his theory of how it had been committed and, a few days later, announced that a red-haired man recently arrested and jailed in Texarkana with a red-haired woman companion was the killer he sought. The redhead also had committed an unsolved murder in another county, he said. He asked for and received from a Grand Jury a special "hurry up" indictment against the redhead and set off to bring him in. But other lawmen in other counties wanted to question the redhead, and he was moved about from one jail to another for a short period of time. Kern did not retrieve him, but he did get the woman. And he announced to newsmen that the woman had confessed that her lover had committed both murders as Kern had theorized.

But a sheriff in Waxahachie, who was holding the redhead, listened to the redhead's story—and checked it out. At the time of both murders, he learned conclusively, the redhead and his woman had been spreading hot checks across Colorado and New Mexico. If any Houston reporter demanded that Kern explain the woman's confession, it was not printed in the newspapers.

On another occasion, Kern and Klevenhagen arrested two men—Diego Carlino and Louis Marino—for the shotgun slaying of a Houston gambler-restaurateur, Vincent Vallone, Sr. They did not take the men directly to the Harris County jail. Instead, each one was taken to a different county and held incommunicado for several days, the arrested men said. During that time, both men later claimed, they were hanged by their necks with their toes barely touching the floor while their captors beat them.

Marino did not confess to the slaying, possibly because Percy Foreman, the lawyer, had been informed that Marino was being held in another county and was stirring up the waters in a hunt for him. Marino was brought hastily to the Harris County jail. Carlino was brought in later, and he had confessed.

That Marino had been mistreated became public knowledge because his parish priest went to the jail and saw raw welts on his neck and other obvious signs of manhandling . . . marks a sane man wouldn't make on himself or ask a friend to put there.

Marino was not indicted or tried in the case, though Kern had called him guilty. Carlino was—and a jury found him not guilty. Kern and Klevenhagen, enraged by the way Attorney Foreman had raked them over the coals during the trial, attacked him in a courthouse corridor even though Foreman was on crutches from an accident.

(Years later a respected Harris County judge commended Foreman in a public meeting, saying the lawyer, by his fearless attacks on police over the decades, had done more than any man, institution or legal act to curtail the practice of taking confessions by force. It was a most unusal statement for a judge to make against the law enforcement establishment.)

I have no opinion on the guilt or innocence of Marino or Carlino, though a jury did. Kern said the redhaired woman confessed that her lover had killed two men—murders he did not commit—and I have no reason to suspect she made the confession because she was mistreated. In the past I had sat on Death Row and heard men from every section of the state claim they had been beaten into making confessions, and I had not believed them. In the future I would hear many other men make the same claim—some of them sent to Death Row by Kern and Klevenhagen—and I would not be able to completely disavow them.

It took no study for me to accept that simple, ignorant men committed more crimes of violence than did sophisticated men of means. And it took but little to realize that when sophisticated men of means did commit crimes of violence they seldom were executed for them. Those who were electrocuted were the blacks, the Mexican-Americans, the poor whites and whites out of favor in their communities for one reason or another having nothing to do with the criminal allegations for which they died.

The old filing case with all the data concerning Death Row inmates was a rich source of information in this regard. Studying the information, absorbing it, making statistical analyses of the cases, brought me to the only possible conclusion: seldom if ever had a man in Texas been sentenced to death for an offense against one of his peers. The victim was, in almost every case, a member of a higher socioeconomic group than the perpetrator.

The records also showed that while most condemned men had been executed for murdering only one person, it had been tolerated for others to kill as many as five persons without paying the supreme price.

These two obvious inequities were almost on par with the "automatic exemption" from the death sentence enjoyed by the women of the state.

"Old Sparky," then, was a social weapon, an instrument of discrimination against black males, Mexican-American males and poor white males. And the frightening thing was my belief that in my home state, a state I loved, a majority of the people wouldn't give a damn about the truth if I wrote it across the sky in letters of fire. Racial and social discrimination were as much a part of Texas as oil and cattle. But to discriminate against a man in his work and everyday life was one thing; to execute him for an offense which did not send his racial or social "betters" to the chair was a crime against heaven.

And from the old filing case emerged one fact that sealed the discrimination verdict: no white man died in the chair for murdering a black, raping a black or robbing a black with firearms . . . and the first of these offenses was a not uncommon occurrence.

Indeed, blacks were not executed for murdering blacks because district attorneys and juries didn't consider the offense a serious one, and newsmen privately referred to such slayings as "misdemeanor murders." Ironically, a black received a stiff sentence for murdering another black only when the jury contained a number of black jurors. In meting out a stiff sentence, the black jurors were trying to elevate the status of the race. They were saying, in effect, "The black who was slain was a human being and thus important —and both he and his slayer should be judged as white men are judged."

I have written that no woman has died in the electric chair in Huntsville prison. True, and only two came close to doing so. But Texans did execute one woman, Chipita Rodriguez, who ran a small roadside inn during the Civil War near San Patricio, Texas.

One night in 1863 a horse trader named John Savage stopped for the night at Chipita's inn. His pockets were jingling with gold, for Savage had sold a herd of horses to the Confederate command. Several days later some women washing clothes in nearby Aransas Creek saw Savage's body floating by.

Chipita Rodriguez was tried for his murder in an adobe hut, and sentenced to death by Judge Ira Nell. The jury that found her guilty recommended mercy, and Ben Thompson, the notorious gunman-gambler, testified as a character witness. But Judge Nell said Chipita had to be hanged from the neck "until all life has fled." He ruled that her boyfriend, one "Little Juan" Silvera, was a minor accomplice in the crime; he gave "Little Juan" five years in prison.

According to the late Ed Kilman, noted Texas newspaperman and historian, "Chipita was bundled into a wagon, seated upon a crude cypress coffin made for her, and hauled out to Robert Weir's pasture. Halting under a giant mesquite tree, the deputy sheriff tossed a rope over a limb above, tied one end around Chipita's neck and the other end around the trunk of the tree. Then he lashed the backs of the mules and they bounded forward, pulling the wagon out from under Chipita. There she dangled, kicking and squirming, until her body relaxed and she hung limp . . . ."

One legend had it, according to Kitmall, that Chipita's ghost so haunted "Little Juan" Silvera—she always wore a noose while visiting him—that his life thereafter was a miserable shambles. Chipita, says the legend, gave up her life for her guilty lover.

Long after her execution it was reported that an old man, on his deathbed, confessed to Sheriff Dave Odem that he, not Chipita, was the killer of John Savage. Perhaps the old man was "Little Juan" Silvera . . . .

Kilman also recorded the case of Pamelia Mann, the most notorious female criminal in the Republic of Texas. Pamelia gained a paragraph in conventional histories because she had been friendly with Sam Houston while she ran an inn at Washington-on-the-Brazos. So friendly that when Houston later was leading his tattered troops in retreat from General Santa Anna, she loaned him a yoke of oxen to pull a cannon. Pamelia thought Houston was trying to escape to safety in Louisiana, a move which she approved. When she learned he intended to stand and fight at San Jacinto—and thereby endanger her oxen—she whipped out a knife and told Houston: "General, you told me a damn lie!" Thereupon she cut the traces attaching her oxen to the cannon, climbed aboard one of the beasts and rode away to safety.

After Houston defeated Santa Anna and gained independence for Texas, Pamelia showed up as manager of the Mansion House, a Houston hotel. Here she became infamous as the most sued and most prosecuted woman in the Republic, with indictments against her ranging from larceny, counterfeiting, assault to kill, adultery and, finally, forgery.

Forgery was a capital offense in the Republic—and

Pamelia was charged with forging the name of William Barrett Travis, an Alamo martyr, on a receipt which was to prove she had paid a $1,000 note.

A jury found her guilty, and the death sentence was mandatory. Judge Ben C. Franklin ordered her hanging. She was lodged in jail to await her doom.

But Pamelia had made many friends among the residents and guests of the Mansion House. They put on the pressure. The next morning the twelve jurors marched into President Mirabeau B. Lamar's office and recommended Pamelia "as a fit subject for executive clemency." The death penalty for forgery, they asserted, was "severe and bordering upon vindictive justice . . . ."

President Lamar knew Pamelia, Kilman wrote, "had probably lunched with her in the Mansion House dining room, and perhaps attended social shindigs there."

He not only commuted the death sentence but proclaimed: "I, Mirabeau B. Lamar, President of the Republic of Texas, do . . . pardon and exonerate the said Pamelia Mann for the said offense of forgery . . . ."

Pamelia Mann beat the noose—and the only two women to reach Death Row or its feminine equivalent beat the electric chair.

One was Emma (Straight Eight) Oliver, a black woman standing close to six feet tall and weighing 170 pounds. She was not a hulking person, but well-proportioned, and she prowled the streets of San Antonio with a leopard's grace as she plied her trade in her teens. Later she moved into a jungle of bawdy houses where she was in great demand.

By the time she was 23, the offense reports of the San Antonio police carried one recorded murder against her. By the time she was 36, six other killings had been chalked up to her, and she had spent several years in prison.

But time, booze and the demands of her profession victimized her. Gone was her lithe dark beauty, dulled were the flecks of gold in her eyes, scarred was her face from a hundred clashes. It took four lines of type in the Department of Corrections report to detail the knife scars that laced her body. And Emma Oliver wound up as a maid in the very brothels that once reverberated to the laughter of her younger, more boisterous years.

The supreme irony of her career was that her eighth and final killing—the one that sent her to Death Row—resulted from a brawl set off by a white man who was molesting the madame of the bawdy house where Emma Oliver worked.

"She just whipped out her knife and carved that man to bits," was the way the district attorney put it to the jury.

But other maids accorded her this accolade: "She was a loyal employee."

She arrived at the Huntsville unit and promptly told the warden she wasn't going to stay on Death Row "with all those men."

The warden hastily assured her this would not be the case. He had converted an old auditor's office in the basement into a personal cell for her. It was plushly furnished compared with Death Row. But the plumbing was slightly out of kilter. Every time she flushed the commode a big "SHOOM" would echo up and down the corridor, and the pipes would rattle throughout the unit.

"Everybody in Huntsville knows when Straight-Eight Emma goes to the john," became a popular saying.

The regular door to the office had been replaced by a door of steel bars, and three matrons were assigned to guard her, each working an eight-hour shift.

She refused to talk to me at any length, though I was able to pass the time of day with her occasionally.

"I ain't talking about it," was her stock comment. "But I'll never die in that chair—I got friends. You just wait and see."

She received the usual, automatic "governor's stay" of thirty days, then two more reprieves and, finally, was scheduled to die. Meantime, forces were working back in San Antonio, where a number of citizens pleaded with Governor Allan Shivers to spare her life. Some clemency petitions contained the names of those who said Emma Oliver had killed to protect another.

This may have helped. But meanwhile it was discovered

that she had an incurable illness. Her sentence was commuted to life and she was transferred to the women's unit at Goree. Two years later she died in the unit hospital. She breathed her last at the exact minute a man named R.J. Hulen went down in the electric chair.

The Fred A. Tones case brought the second woman to Death Row. Tones was a 44-year-old businessman who got involved with a couple of unusual characters—Carolyn Ann Lima and Leslie Ashley. The latter was a sometime female impersonator.

The case got underway publicly when a passing citizen noticed a man's body burning in a ditch in Houston's East End. The body was identified as that of Tones. Missing was his white Lincoln convertible. Police soon put out an all-points bulletin for two suspects. FBI agents arrested Carolyn Lima and Leslie Ashley in New York City. Ashley was dressed as a woman.

It was a shocking story that emerged from the police investigation, statements of the two principals, and from the witness stand as the two were tried for murder. Carolyn was eighteen at the time, Ashley was 21.

Carolyn, as a part-time prostitute, had visited Tones' office weekly for some time. On the day of the murder, Ashley accompanied her, and it became a "three-way date" according to trial testimony.

Carolyn testified that Tones began abusing her, that Ashley tried to pull Tones away from her. Ashley testified Tones "began hitting me, and then he was choking me . . . he was hitting my head against the window, and I thought I was going to die any minute." Carolyn said Tones was shouting "I'll kill both of you!"

Ashley said he got a pistol from Carolyn's handbag and it went off in the scuffle, then fell from his hand to the floor.

Carolyn said she snatched up the gun and blasted Tones five times. "He was acting like he was going to kill one of us, and then the other, and I kept begging him to stop but he wouldn't," Carolyn testified. "I just pulled the trigger, and I froze to it and kept on pulling it."

Carolyn and Ashley loaded Tones' body into the trunk of the Lincoln, hauled it to the ditch where it had been found, then soaked it with gasoline.

"I set fire to him and he lit up like a Christmas tree," Carolyn told reporters at Houston's International Airport upon her return from New York in the custody of police officers.

A jury found the pair guilty of murder. Then began a long series of appeals by their attorneys for a new trial. While Ashley languished on Death Row and Carolyn was kept in the Goree unit under special guard, they were made ever hopeful as legal maneuver after legal maneuver finally got the case before the U.S. Fifth Circuit Court of Appeals in New Orleans. And this court handed down what is considered an historic ruling.

The Court granted Carolyn and Ashley a new trial on the grounds that Harris County District Attorney Frank Briscoe had denied the pair a fair trial by failing to notify defense attorneys there was evidence that Leslie Ashley was insane.

The Court said the district attorney's silence "amounts to such fundamental unfairness in the trial of a criminal case as to amount to almost a denial of due process."

(A dissenting judge said the defense should have asked about the outcome of a psychiatric examination, that the district attorney had not refused the information—he simply had not volunteered it.)

New trials were set for the pair, and they were tried separately. Carolyn went to trial first. And she changed her testimony. She told the jury it was Leslie Ashley who pumped all six shots from the pistol into Tones, and that it was Ashley who poured gasoline over Tones' body and set it afire. She said she was afraid of Leslie, that he had threatened to kill her if she refused to say she fired five of the six shots.

Carolyn's attorney, Clyde Woody, wound up his summation to the jury by declaring, "They want you to take this little girl by the hand and walk her down a long hall to that little green door!"

The jury considered, then gave Carolyn a five-year sentence on a murder-without-malice charge. The judge gave her credit for three years "jail time."

She was returned to Goree after assuring reporters there would be no more "hanky-panky" in her life. She was released a year later to assume a continuation of a Texas tradition.

Leslie Ashley had three sanity hearings. He was held in the prison system for seven years, then freed. (The state forgot to inform Houston police of all the developments in the Lima-Ashley case; in 1972 Ashley was stopped for a minor traffic infraction, then held in jail because the desk clerk discovered a notation in police files asking that a "Leslie Ashley" be held for investigation in a murder case.)

Texas is not the only state where judges, jurors and governors have grown faint-hearted when considering the ultimate penalty for women.

Only 32 women have been executed nationwide since 1930, and none since 1962. Meantime, 2,958 men were electrocuted, hanged, gassed or shot. Yet, as my friend had pointed out, women commit about 25 percent of the murders in the country. In Houston, for example, police detected 203 murders in 1972, and women were the killers in 41 (or 20 percent) of them. None was given the death penalty.

Woman's role as Mother, and vestiges of Southern Chivalry, no doubt account for much of the immunity women enjoy. But neither keeps men from murdering women or, for that matter, women from murdering women. It appears that only when men are in the jury box they recall the chivalrous days and reflect on woman's role in propagation and child-rearing.

Earlier I had accepted as fact the argument that punishment—or rather, the fear of capital punishment—was a deterrent, that the execution of one man would keep another man from murder, rape or armed robbery.

By the time I completed my investigations I had concluded that man had always promoted capital punishment as a deterrent simply to justify the use of it. Actually, he cares little whether capital punishment deters or fosters homicide.

He favors it primarily because he hates and fears the killer and wants his blood. He won't admit this publicly—and he likely never will.

To his credit, man cannot help feeling this hate and fear of the violent criminal simply because he is human. He discredits himself by hiding these real emotions and promoting capital punishment as a deterrent.

The murder most detested is the premeditated one. So let us assume that Smith wants to murder Jones. He lies in wait for Jones in the darkness. He swings his knife at Jones to kill him, but as he swings he stumbles. The knife tears into Jones' body but misses the heart by an inch. Jones lives.

What happens to Smith?

He receives a short prison sentence, if anything, for attempted murder or assault.

Why? Why don't we execute Smith? He had the intent to kill. He had malice in his heart. And, if not executed, he may try again.

If we say we favor capital punishment because it is a deterrent, we would execute Smith. It would be the logical thing to do.

But logic has nothing to do with it. We do not execute Smith simply because he has not aroused our hate and fear enough. He fulfills all of the logical requirements for us to execute him but not the emotional ones.

At one point during my studies Frances came into the den and asked me, "How will you ever be sure that capital punishment is not a deterrent? There are no statistics on the persons who may have been kept from murder because of the fear of capital punishment. How will you ever know if there were one or a dozen? Or a thousand? Or none at all?"

I couldn't know. The statistics were on the persons I knew were not deterred—the ones I had seen on Death Row, and the hundreds of thousands of others who had committed murder and had been executed or imprisoned for it. Added to them were those who had killed and left the courtroom free men. And those who had killed but were not captured. And on top of them were those who had killed but who had disguised the murder as an accidental or natural death—and they were legion, according to the best authorities . . . 5,000 annually in the United States alone.

None of them—none—was deterred by anything.

I couldn't know the statistics on those who had been deterred from murder by the fear of capital punishment, but I knew by now that all men are potential killers—all who can pull a trigger, lift a club or swing a knife.

I knew that the insane among us were not deterred from murder by fear of capital punishment simply because they were insane.

Among the sane were those who killed in a flash of fury or fear, and it could not be said with any conviction that the thought of capital punishment ever entered their heads. And the vast majority of slayings were committed under just such circumstances. In the family kitchen. In the corner tavern. The trysting place.

The comparative few who planned murder were convinced they would not be detected, or were willing to gamble that they wouldn't. Some gambled even further—that if they were detected, they would not get the death sentence or might beat the rap entirely.

For the robber or burglar who carried a gun, the situation was the same. He was not deterred by the thought of capital punishment. He took a calculated risk. If he had the pistol only as a threat, he might kill in blind panic. If he were more cold-blooded, he might kill to escape recognition, gambling that he wouldn't be caught. In any event, he took the pistol with him knowing that he might have to use it.

But all men—good and bad, brilliant and stupid—have no fear of death in some cloudy future. The only death we fear is imminent death. Only if each citizen went about his daily life with the state holding a cocked pistol to his head ready to be fired upon provocation would we be deterred.

During my investigations I sometimes would hear someone say, "If they'd just take that son of a bitch out on the main street of town and hang him where everybody could see it, it would damn well stop all this killing and robbing!" History shows that such a remark springs from ignorance.

Public executions were halted in the United States and

abroad because they stimulated criminal activity. When a crowd gathered to watch the execution of a thief, other thieves looted shops and homes at will. Counterfeiters passed their false coins to excited citizens who waited to see a counterfeiter hang. In 1822 the *Yorktown Gazette*, commenting on a Pennsylvania public hanging, concluded: "What has taken place . . . would lead one to believe that the spectacle of a public execution produces less reformation than criminal propensity. While one old offense was atoned for, more than a dozen new ones were committed, and some of a capital grade. Twenty-eight persons were committed to jail for divers offenses . . . such as murder, larceny, assault and battery, besides many gentlemen lost their pocketbooks, though the pickpockets escaped, or the jail would have overflowed . . . ."

I have written flatly that capital punishment or the threat of it does not deter. If in some few cases it *has* deterred, I thank God. But at the same time I deplore the deaths of the executed innocent—and as long as capital punishment is the law of an imperfect state, we run the awful risk of killing innocent men . . . men who confess to crimes they didn't commit because they are tortured . . . men who are poorly represented in court and get the death sentence when a lesser sentence would have been fair and proper . . . men who are discriminated against for racial or social reasons . . . .

Texas, of course, is not the only imperfect state in the Union. In South Carolina, Roger Dedmond was convicted for the murder of his wife; a year later he was released when Lee Roy Martin, the "Gaffney Strangler," confessed to the slaying. In Florida, Robert Watson was convicted of homicide; he was freed because John Frasca, the *Tampa Tribune*'s Pulitzer Prize winning reporter, investigated and found the real killer. In Pennsylvania, three teenagers were found guilty of murder and served sixteen years before a conscientious judge—after a long, intensive investigation—ruled that the murder "never occurred." In Georgia, James Foster was twice identified by a widow as her husband's slayer, and was sentenced to death; two years later a former policeman confessed to the crime. In Washington, D.C., Charles Bernstein was within minutes of his execution when his sentence was commuted. Two years later police proved him innocent of the crime for which he had been convicted, and he received a Presidential pardon. And so it goes . . . .

My research and investigation, then, had convinced me that the death sentence was inequitably handed down and inequitably imposed; that the death sentence or the threat of it was not a deterrent; that with capital punishment on the books we stood in constant danger of executing the innocent and, indeed, had done so in the past.

And one night in my den my thoughts went back to Buster Northern, as they so often did. He had stomped to death an old woman, but I hadn't wanted him to die for it. I couldn't blame "society" for Northern's conduct; "blaming society" was a pitch I had decried too often when the liberals used it for every ill mankind endured. But it was inescapable that Northern's background had made him what he was, a youngster entirely lacking in moral sensibility until he arrived at Death Row, where he found friends and reached for God.

Others had wanted Northern to die for his crime. They had told themselves that to execute him would stay another's hand from murder. Some had spoken in good faith but honest error. The rest had wanted his blood to rid the world of something they hated and feared. They had wanted revenge, but could not admit it.

Could I make a moral judgment on these people who had reacted instinctively to outrageous murder? My own fists still clenched the moment I heard or read of a brutal assault.

Tears came into my eyes. There in my den I was agonizing over every human being who had lived on this earth. There *was* a moral judgment to be made . . . on all of us. There was a moral judgment to be made on me, Don Reid. At that moment my heart cried out for every condemned man I had "eased into" death; I begged each man's forgiveness for not having fought to save his life.

It was a sad and terrifying thing to look back on important minutes of my life with bitterness and profound regret. But sitting there, my cigar unlit, I determined to bend my best efforts to rid my state and country of capital punishment.

I want to say this quickly and have done with it: no angel visited me with a message from on high. God did not speak to me. Jesus Christ did not lay His hand on mine. But in my den that night the corrosion was swabbed off my heart in a gentle stroke and I became my brother's keeper. I was a Christian. I wanted to live my life as Jesus had said I should. I believed in Him. I believed in Him as much or more than any euphoric Death Row inmate preparing to die. I wanted to *live* for Jesus—and for my fellow man.

I wasn't a nut. I still wanted people to pay their bills at the *Item.* I wanted fair treatment from the town's merchants and others. I could take a drink, smoke a cigar, fall victim to all the evils the flesh is heir to. But I was a better human being who believed in the Word of God. I did not become naive. I did not, I am convinced, become obnoxious to those around me by parading my faith.

And I had made up my mind I would not use Christianity in my fight against capital punishment. Logic would suffice, I had told myself, or at least it should—if I could present it correctly.

I have held to that stand.

7

Commitment

My interview with Buster Northern and the story of his execution created a demand for interviews with and stories about other condemned men, and during the long months of my study and investigation I had satisfied that demand. An editor who saw a story coming over the Associated Press wire with my byline on it knew that another execution was coming up.

These stories, in turn, had created requests for my appearance before civic, service and religious groups. I had ignored them. But now with my decision to fight capital punishment, I saw these requests as opportunities to wage the battle. So I hit the "luncheon circuit" around the state.

I planned my speeches carefully. I was showman enough to know that I must "hook" my audiences with some Death House stories before I settled in to make my pitch for the abolition of capital punishment. And my pitch was low key; I simply pointed out the defects in the administration of justice that could lead a man to death, and added to that my conviction that the threat of capital punishment was no deterrent.

I was naive. I had misjudged my fellow Texans . . . or a majority of them. They reveled in the grim details of the "last mile," and if the condemned man fought his way to the chair—or was dragged to it kicking and screaming—they loved it even more.

But they looked at me with suspicion when I discussed the flaws in the system of justice, and their jaws tightened when I told them bluntly that capital punishment was not a deterrent, that it never had been, and that other methods of punishment were superior . . . and cheaper.

Their ears were closing by the time I began describing successful rehabilitation programs, new methods of crime prevention and detection. And I had lost them for good by the time I began quoting statistics which established that more murders per capita were committed in death penalty states than in states that had abandoned capital punishment.

Had they not been, for the most part, decent people, I would have loomed as the enemy in their eyes. Instead, they relaxed and pitied me for my stupidity.

I had not counted on the staying power of the Old Testament exhortations. My facts shattered against a stubborn belief in "an eye for an eye." Often it was said to me, "The only good murderer is a dead murderer."

But my speaking engagements did not decrease in number. Texans were still eager to hear "electrocution stories," and were willing to put up with my heresies to hear them. So I plodded on, sprinkling the circuit with blood and thunder in order to try to sell my beliefs. In after-speech sessions I was often given the "old buddy" treatment—"Aw, come on now, old buddy, you know you don't believe that kind of stuff. What would you do if somebody killed your wife?"

On the circuit I made a talk to a large group of Episcopalians. A few days later I received a copy of their monthly journal. On the front page was a story under the heading, "Death For Criminals." The first sentence of the story said, "Capital punishment is a necessary institution in the United States today." It was a long story, continued to the back page in a column next to a report on my talk. And the story on my talk ended with the reporter's comment: "Because of Reid's personal involvement, many of his listeners felt that it was impossible for him to form any clear opinion without allowing his emotions to place him in a biased position . . . ."

I let out a long sigh; the reporter probably had never studied a page about capital punishment, never sat in a courtroom during a murder trial, never served on a jury in a capital case, never participated in handing down a death sentence. It likely never had occurred to him that the electric chair was a social weapon, and he would not have entertained the premise if the facts were chiseled into his sidewalk where he saw them daily.

Postcards and letters came to my desk in a constant stream. Cards such as these:

"If a man killed one of your loved ones, for no reason at all, you would not be so ready to turn a bunch of murderers loose on the public to kill and kill again. It is people like you and the sob sisters that has ruined our country and made it unsafe for the law-abiding people. The Bible says (not once but in several places) that when a person kills, he shall be stoned until dead. And you want to turn them out to kill again. If they break one of our laws they should be punished for it. I heard an ex-con say it was so much better in prison than outside, and that he was going back and he did. So it is no wonder we have so much crime in this country."

"I wonder if you have prayed for or visited the victims of these killers. Do you console their children? I know one thing: once electrocuted they will never kill again. Please consider your values again."

"Before you die you will become one of the most despised men of society because of your sympathy for an inhuman creature, born in an inhuman family and that mercilessly killed a poor old lady in order to rob her and caused you to become an odious bleeding heart that has sympathy for criminals, instead of sympathy for the victims of criminals. You shall roast in hell unless you become able to have sympathy for the victims of the criminals. There is no hope for you, Mr. Reid."

"Maybe you should stand by and watch as a long line of little girls are raped and strangled to death, then you probably wouldn't feel too badly about the executions. This country has gone from hanging without a trial to practically no punishment at all. This country will end up becoming a communist state, and a communist country will not tolerate the lawlessness we have in this country."

"Mr. Reid, I beg your pardon for asking this pointed question, which is this, if you were to go home and find your wife or daughter criminally assaulted and murdered, don't you think you would want the criminal put to death? I surely would, if it were to happen in my family. Such criminals usually repeat when allowed to go free after a few years in prison have been served."

Released murderers and rapists repeat their crimes far less often than other convicted men. Convicted murderers, in fact, are considered more responsive to rehabilitation than all other prison inmates. It is only when a paroled killer does it again that the public accuses parole officials of "turning killers loose on the streets like mad dogs." Forgers, who rarely if ever carry guns, lead the national list of "repeaters." Auto thieves, robbers, burglars, those convicted of assault, those convicted of fraud, and gamblers follow in that order.

"We never had men like Sirhan Sirhan or Oswald years ago! They know that the most they can get is life in prison, a roof over their heads, three meals a day, clean beds to sleep in, nothing to want for. Where else can they get mothered like that?"

"If one of the little bastards had murdered one of your loved ones, how would you feel? The heartbreak of good, law-abiding citizens has been brought about for no other reason than a crazy man was turned loose on the world. I say let them burn!"

"Don't you know why God said to stone them to death for murder, rape, adultery and even a son who cursed, drank or wouldn't help his parents? You haven't thoroughly read your Bible. It wasn't for revenge or punishment, it was to remove the evil from Israel."

"I would like you to know there are many people in the world—in prisons and outside, as well—and it all falls back on the shoulders of the parents of the lawbreakers. It falls on the churches even harder than on the person as he was not taught God's law and principles."

"You're a sissy, Mr. Reid, I would have no compunctions about watching an execution. They deserve the most horrible fate we can devise."

"I sat on three murder trial juries and we convicted all three and gave them the death penalty and I think nothing about it."

"You must be a savage beast yourself. They shoot rabid animals and they should do the same with savages who commit these crimes."

"God bless you, Mr. Reid. You are an angel on earth, and He must have sent you here to help guide us to the right way of thinking."

"It is a surprise to me that this, the largest state, has people so barbarian in their views. It seems a shame that people allow their lust for blood or revenge or hate to carry them so far. This idea of death as a deterrent is an excuse. No matter what, if a person is going to kill, at the time he is doing it he is not going to consider the outcome. The urge to kill is in everyone of us. Some suppress and control it better than others."

"We share your profound convictions. In discussions with others on the subject, however, we have felt the need for factual information to strengthen our position. Could you send us names of possible sources to whom we could write for data and statistics?"

"After your talk, the thought that stuck in my mind was your statement, 'But for the grace of God, there go I.' You are so right. Many of us (and I am but a country minister) have in our own way failed some of these underprivileged, and as a consequence they have become hardened criminals."

"If I was ever uncertain of my convictions against capital punishment, I'm not uncertain now! And even though we may not meet personally in this life, I want by this means to say my thanks to you. Your courage, compassion and convictions of right inspire me."

In my mail one morning was a request for "just a few lines" about myself from the program chairman of a businessmen's group I was to address in an East Texas town. He needed the few lines in order to introduce me properly, he wrote. "I want to give you a good build-up!"

"Hell—I'm just an entertainer!" I said aloud to myself. "I'm a curiosity, that's all!"

I knew I was a businessman. I had payrolls to meet and professional responsibilities to the *Item*'s readers and advertisers, personal responsibilities to my wife and the two children born to us.

I sat down at my typewriter and wrote the Master of Ceremonies just who Don Reid was, my battered ego throbbing with every tap on the keys. I was a respected man in Texas journalism. I had served as president of the Texas Gulf Coast Press Association. I had been vice president then president of the Texas chapter of Sigma Delta Chi, the professional journalism society. My newspaper was a force in civic and political efforts in the state. I had received more than a dozen journalism awards of consequence. I had been a consultant in the preparation of prize-winning radio and television documentaries. And I was a Sunday School teacher at the First Methodist Church of Huntsville.

That, by thunder, was who Don Reid was!

I mailed the "few lines" with an indignant flourish. An hour or more passed before my anger passed and embarrassment took its place. And with the embarrassment came the realization that I had, to a great extent, been spinning my wheels with my speeches . . . I could never make enough speeches to gain enough converts to turn the tide against capital punishment.

What I needed to do was join a group of dedicated people who would take the fight to the seat of government . . . to the legislature, where the law could be scrubbed from the books. But could I afford to do that? My readers and advertisers had not criticized me for my speeches on the luncheon circuit. Perhaps they even had smiled and winked at my activities. But joining a formal organization to carry on the fight might be another matter in their eyes. Such a step would brand me as a "soft-headed liberal." No longer would I be a lone knight-errant with a dull lance and a spavined horse. I would be one of those "professional bleeding hearts" so despised—and apparently feared—by the status quoers.

I talked it over with Frances at dinner. That is, I talked while she ate and listened. There was a soft smile on her face before I finished my worried presentation.

"What's the smile for?" I asked. "This is a serious proposition.

She laughed. "Serious, my angel food cake! Why don't you go ahead and call Harry McCormick in Dallas. You know he's been wanting to organize a group like that for years." She waved a roll at me. "Go on. Call him."

Harry McCormick was a fine newspaperman for the Dallas *News*. He had received his early training with the Scripps-Howard Newspaper Alliance and later had been a crime reporter for other Texas newspapers before going to the *News*. He would come down to Huntsville occasionally to report on prison administration, and almost every time we would get into long discussions about capital punishment.

Now, on the phone, I told him I was ready to make a concrete move to form a group to rid the state of capital punishment. He was elated. And he told me that Father Francis Duffy, the prison chaplain with whom I had spent many a pre-execution night in Death Row, was eager to participate in such a movement. Father Duffy, he reminded me, was now pastor of St. Mary's Cathedral in San Antonio.

He also told me that an associate professor of philosophy at the University of Texas, Dr. John Silber, was anxious to form such a group. "We four are enough to get it started, Don," McCormick said. "Let's get together in Austin in January so we can plan to argue at the March session of the legistature. There's pressure on for an abolition bill. In the meantime, be thinking of ideas."

I said I would. But before I could get into gear, a writer, Ernest Havemann, came to see me. He wanted my help on an article he was preparing for *Reader's Digest* on capital punishment. The article would be entitled, "Capital Punishment Is Not The Answer," in anticipation of the execution of Caryl Chessman in California. The Chessman case, of course, had created an international furor.

I thought this work could be more important than "getting

ideas" for our Texas organization, and McCormick agreed. I worked with Havemann on the article. Then the magazine's advertising agency asked me to come to New York to help promote it. I received a bit of publicity myself in New York, enough that the National Broadcasting Company asked me to stop in Washington, D.C., on my return trip to Texas. When I arrived I was told I was to appear on a panel show with FBI Director J. Edgar Hoover and two NBC newsmen. The subject: capital punishment.

I had mixed feelings about Hoover. I respected him as a loyal, talented public servant on the one hand. On the other, I felt he had built a publicity machine inside the FBI to promote himself to Homeric stature. And I had wondered about something. During the long years he had been preaching about the "Communist menace" he had ignored organized crime until the mobsters literally had the country's economy by the throat. Indeed, he had indicated doubt of the Mafia's existence even after the Kefauver Committee had definitely established it. (It would be some years before FBI agents would become members of task forces dedicated to the Mafia's extinction.)

On the show I found him to be, as my mother would have said, "a nice man." He had a high regard for his opinions, and he stated flatly that capital punishment was a deterrent. He did not indicate that he felt this ended all debate, but I somehow got the impression he believed it should.

He argued that had an act similar to the Lindberg Act been on the law books, the kidnapping of the famous flyer's son would not have occurred. The act, passed after the kidnapping, made the death penalty mandatory for kidnapping.

I pointed out that many kidnappings had occurred since passage of the act, and I argued that honest law enforcement and quick trials were by far a better method of deterring crime.

Not so, Hoover said. There would be more crime without capital punishment.

The figures compiled by his own statisticians proved the contrary, I countered.

Back and forth it went. I concluded with the remarks that the FBI's own work supported my argument that use of modern investigative techniques, and speedy trials with prosecutors holding unassailable evidence, was the answer to a rising crime rate. I told Hoover that many convicts had told me, "You can beat the state courts but you can't beat Uncle Sam. Those investigations by FBI agents are so thorough that the case is already made for the prosecutor before the trial opens."

Hoover smiled. "Thank you for those kind words," he said.

We had agreed on one point—that state courts should emulate federal courts in the matter of presentencing investigations that provided federal judges with vital information not brought out in the courtroom.

We shook hands on parting, and he sent me an autographed copy of his latest book about the Communists. We corresponded irregularly after that, and at my request he sent one of his top aides, Carter DeLoach, to Houston to speak to a meeting of the Texas Gulf Coast Press Association.

When I returned to Texas the four of us—McCormick, Father Duffy, Dr. Silber and I—met in Austin to found the Texas Society to Abolish Capital Punishment. Dr. Silber was named president, McCormick and Father Duffy vice-presidents, and I was made the secretary. We had no treasurer because we had no money.

I helped Dr. Silber prepare a mailing piece on our purposes and plans, and these were sent to people we knew or suspected shared our views. They were expected to pass the literature around to their friends in the effort to obtain membership.

Within a year we had grown from the original four officers to about 140 members. Membership cost $2 a year, and a life membership cost $10. We eventually achieved a budget large enough to pay for letterheads, envelopes and the stamps to mail them.

The small, reluctant growth didn't surprise us. The climate was changing on the subject of capital punishment, but not enough to gain any popular support. We found that people in the public eye, people who might normally be expected to support significant social and civic movements or causes, just weren't interested in becoming card-carrying members of the Texas Society to Abolish Capital Punishment.

The time for the hearing for which we were preparing finally arrived. The hearing was before the House Criminal Jurisprudence Committee. To be debated was the proposed Bridges-Whitfield bill to outlaw capital punishment. The debate lasted five hours.

One of the principal sections of the bill would have required those convicted of capital crimes to serve a minimum of fifteen years before they would become eligible for parole. Juries under the proposal could recommend that longer minimums could be given, and the courts would have the authority to carry out jury recommendations.

College professors, district attorneys, sheriffs, ministers and newspapermen testified. The thrust of the proponents of the death penalty was that society needed to be protected from "amoral individuals" who often "deserved to be put to death." Opponents of capital punishment argued that it was not administered justly, that "it has no place in a Christian and democratic society," and that it had failed in its declared purpose to deter crime.

Dr. Silber made an hour-long statement. He presented detailed statistics on the incidence of murder in states which had abolished capital punishment in comparison with those which had not, and added: "Some remarkable facts stand out. First, the homicide rate in abolition states is consistently less than half as large as in death penalty states. Second, the average number of executions per year in the last four years (prior to 1961) has decreased to less than one third of the average of the 1930s, although the population has increased by forty million.

"If the death penalty were a necessary deterrent," he testified, "we should expect murders to increase as the number of executions decrease, and we should expect the homicide rate to be higher in states that have abolished capital punishment than in the states that have retained it. But precisely the opposite has happened."

In my testimony, I cited the case of a man who had been serving a thirty-year murder sentence in Oklahoma. He had been released shortly before the hearing began when another convict in Texas confessed to the crime for which he had been imprisoned.

"The man they incarcerated up there," I testified, "had pleaded guilty. He was an alcoholic and didn't know whether or not he had committed the crime. They said to him, 'Either you plead guilty and we'll give you thirty years or else we'll give you the chair.' I guess it's lucky for him he pleaded guilty."

During the course of the hearing I noted the lack of even basic information by legislators arguing for and against retention of the death penalty. In one instance, a legislator made the statement that the racial proportions of those executed in Texas since 1924 were "about even." I knew that between 1924 and the date of the hearing 216 blacks, 23 Mexican-Americans and 101 whites had been executed. I felt that common intelligence would prohibit a state legislator from making such a statement. The whites totaled only thirty percent of those executed.

Another legislator, Tom Andrews of Aransas Pass, took issue with Fred Schmidt, an official of the AFL-CIO, when the latter testified that the death penalty did not offer a "fair shake" to the poor and the ignorant. Andrews insisted that "as a lawyer, I know this state goes to great lengths to provide attorneys for poor defendants." This was obviously untrue. Witness Schmidt replied that in all cases there was "a direct ratio between the ability to pay and the quality of counsel in our courtrooms."

Another legislator asked Schmidt if it wasn't true "that the crime rate for capital crimes is largest among lower income groups?" Schmidt said that might be true for armed robbery "because there are more people in the lower income brackets." But he added that he was sure this would not hold true "in cases of crimes of passion, like murder."

Whereupon, the legislator asked, "Isn't it true the people in the lower income brackets are usually the unemployed and have more time for crimes of passion?"

Mr. Schmidt retorted, "How about people who are retired or are so rich they don't have to work for a living. Do they have more time for crimes of passion?"

I had recommended that life in prison should be the ultimate penalty for murder. Representative Frank McGregor countered that this would cost the taxpayers too much. McGregor said at the time that it cost the state's taxpayers more to take care of a prisoner "than it does to get a room in a hotel with three meals a day . . . it costs about $12 per day per man." As a matter of fact, it cost the state less than $4 per day per man.

In another exchange, Truman Roberts, representing the District and County Attorneys Association, argued that society had "enacted around ourselves a fence of law," and the bill would put a hole in that fence. He insisted a mandatory life sentence would not work, that governors and parole boards might commute or lessen prison terms at any time. But later, questioned on the source of his statements that the death penalty for armed robbery in the 1930s had caused a decrease in that crime, Roberts admitted he had no statistics, but did "have the word of veteran police officers" on the subject. Asked by a legislator if he believed capital punishment was a deterrent to crime, Roberts replied, "I do, I certainly do." Asked for back-up statistics, Roberts said he had none, "but I've talked to people who've told me that very thing." When Representative Stanford Smith asked Roberts if he preferred exclusion by killing or by permanent removal (life in prison), Roberts replied it would be difficult to assure permanent removal, adding, "It's also a more expensive proposition for the state."

Representative Bob Eckhardt, chairman of the hearing (now a U.S. Congressman), pointed out that eight men had been executed in Texas in the past year, and asked Roberts, "Should this little savings (financial) be weighed against the entire moral issue?" Roberts replied that life-term prisoners, "with no hope of release, might create a hard core of inmates in the prison and cause a hard problem." Roberts also said the testimony of prison wardens on the undesirability of the death penalty should not carry weight since "wardens would tend to view such men with more compassion."

Then the Reverend Robert Ingram of Houston's St. Thomas Episcopal Church contended "that at stake here is the questioning of a system of justice used throughout Christianity and Western Civilization for centuries. *Lex Taliones* is still the concept of justice for Christians—'an eye for an eye, a tooth for a tooth.' Retaliation . . . I don't know if that's the right word . . . retribution is an end in itself." He concluded by quoting St. Paul that the state is "the minister of God's wrath." Representative Eckhardt quoted John Adams: "It is more important to save one innocent man even if ten guilty men go free," and asked Reverend Ingram if he agreed. The minister replied, "No. I think that's absurd."

That's the way the hearing went—facts and figures on the one side failing to penetrate a wall of ignorance and Old Testament exhortations. The bill did not pass. Capital punishment remained on the books.

I did not escape that day unscathed. After the hearing, as I walked down the stately capitol steps, I heard someone calling my name. A newsman who covered the capitol beat for a Central Texas newspaper approached me. I had known him for fifteen years. We shook hands and I gave him a cigar. He said he had been surprised to see me testify at the hearing.

He shook his head. "I don't see how you could honestly make a pitch for abolition after that Humpy Ross deal at Huntsville," he said. "Are you going to tell me that Ross' sentence should have been commuted to life? Or that he should have been confined in a mental hospital?"

"Yes, that's what I'm going to tell you."

He examined my face, trying to read doubt in my eyes. Then he changed the subject and in a few moments was off to cover his beat.

I stood there on the steps and thought of Humpy Ross. Herman Lee (Humpy) Ross, a hunchbacked gnome of a black man. Four feet, ten inches tall with powerful arms that reached his knees and ended in hands as large as eggplants. Tubercular with a pockmarked face. Ugly, angry, full of hatred for everything in life.

Ross was condemned to die for the murder of a Galveston liquor store owner during a holdup attempt. He escaped the Galveston County jail, and in a wild running gun battle with lawmen he killed one officer and wounded another. Recaptured, he was brought under heavy guard to Huntsville.

On Death Row Ross prowled his iron cage like a horror-movie spider. He refused to talk to anyone—to the chaplains, guards or the warden. And one day he sent a wave of fear throughout the entire prison system.

An elderly guard, M.L. Rucker, stooped to slide a tray of food through the slot in Ross' cell. Suddenly Ross erupted. His huge hands flashed through the bars and grabbed Rucker's head. The powerful arms banged Rucker's skull forward against the bars. The hands tore and ripped at the guard's face and eyes.

Other occupants of Death Row, galvanized into a frenzy by Rucker's screams of pain and terror, strained against their cell doors in a vain effort to see what was going on.

Into this madhouse came a notorious old Texas outlaw, Pete McKenzie. In his younger days McKenzie had killed three men, including a San Antonio policeman. His latest sentence—death—had been commuted, and he was working the Death Row cellblock as a janitor or "building tender." For this job he carried a huge ring of keys.

McKenzie quickly saw that if he grabbed Rucker's feet to pull him away from the cell door the guard's neck might snap in Ross' fearsome grasp. Calmly he sorted through the keys on the big ring until he found the key to Ross's cell. Ross, by now completely berserk and intent on destroying Rucker, ignored McKenzie as the old outlaw slipped into the cell.

With all of his strength, McKenzie swung the heavy key ring against Ross' head. Ross wouldn't let go of Rucker's head. He cackled in wild glee as he jerked the guard's head against the cell bars.

McKenzie went to work as methodically as a roustabout driving a tent stake. Again and again he smashed Ross with the keys until at last the madman's grip loosened and he sank to the floor, unconscious. Blood from his head flowed into the blood of his unconscious victim.

McKenzie calmly left the cell and phoned the hospital for help for both men.

On his execution day Ross was feverish. A drainage tube protruded from his body. He had never let me talk to him before and he made no exception on this final day.

In the Death House we could hear Ross' shouts and shrieks from Death Row, muffled by the little green door. Then the door burst open. Ross, fighting and cursing, was dragged into the Death House by three sweating, straining guards. His face was a gargoyle.

His small, burning eyes swung around and took in the warden and the witnesses. He stopped struggling. And it seemed as if that small room would explode when he shouted, "You motherfuckers! I hate you all!"

His eyes settled on me. As the guards wrestled him toward the electric chair, Ross broke loose from them. He lunged for me, his long arms and big hands reaching for my throat. I jumped back, and just before his hands touched me the guards collapsed on him. They picked him up and literally hurled him into the chair. I was sweating and my heart raced.

Once, as the guards were strapping him in, Ross tore loose one hand and ripped at the heavy strap around his waist. A guard grabbed the arm and lashed it to the armrest. One guard held his head while another rammed cotton into Ross' nostrils. Ross was still struggling and cursing when the warden nodded his head and the executioner sent the 1,800 volts through the twisted body.

And then, the strangest aftermath. A halo of crackling electrical fire danced over Ross' head in the haze of smoke and steam. As it flickered out, a visiting policeman broke the stunned silence. "I guess that's what you call hellfire and damnation," he said softly.

Standing on the capitol steps, I remembered that I had filed my story—stripped of most of the terrible details—and had gone home to sit in silence before my piano, my hands resting on the keys. There had been no music for me or Humpy Ross.

Sitting there, I wondered if anyone had ever loved Humpy Ross during his entire life—and if Humpy Ross had ever loved another creature.

Now, on the capitol steps, I couldn't really say what should have been done with Humpy Ross the madman. But aside from all the facts and figures, my heart told me capital punishment was not the answer.

8

And They Kept on Dying

The Austin hearing, of course, prompted no celebration for the charter members of the Texas Society to Abolish Capital Punishment. It did reveal to us that ignorance and suspicion can erect walls almost impervious to assault. Sitting in our hotel suite for a post-hearing meeting, we agreed we had to abandon rhetoric—the weapon the opposition had employed so successfully. We would search out hard facts and figures—statistics, if you will—which could not be denied. So armed, we could go to the people via the speaking circuit and the statewide news media. We could create a receptive climate of knowledge and understanding. Yes, we agreed, we could do all of that.

I returned to Huntsville—and reality. The "future book" in my desk drawer showed a number of executions scheduled within the next ninety days. The state was continuing to kill people.

First on the list was Fred Leath, a forty-year-old window trimmer. He was a well-built, blue-eyed six-footer and a bonafide hero of World War II. He had been awarded the Bronze Star with an oak-leaf cluster, the Purple Heart with two oak-leaf clusters, and his outfit had twice won Distinguished Unit Medals. All proof that Fred Leath had served his country with valor.

But Fred Leath was a homosexual. And he was a homosexual who had killed a fifteen-year-old boy. The youth was a physical fitness buff who spent his time lifting weights and playing pool while Leath supported him. During a scuffle, Leath shot and killed the youth in what he claimed was self-defense.

The prosecuting attorney had called Leath "an odious thing." The jurors had recoiled and handed down the death sentence.

I began an investigation which was hampered by my heavy work schedule. Leath, I learned, came from a family of nine children. His father, Leath told the prison psychiatrist, "was cruel, mean and crazy." His homosexual tendency had not evidenced itself until during the war when he met a man as lonely and friendless as himself. After the war, Leath told the psychiatrist, he suffered periods of depression. His record showed he had served a brief sentence on an assault-to-murder charge in 1958, a dozen years after the war. Some of his Fort Worth acquaintances said Leath was one of the rare homosexuals who "wouldn't play dead" when some "straight" wanted trouble.

When I talked with Leath he said he never had a chance to tell his side of the story to any person in authority. "Not in court or anywhere else," he said. "It was a kangaroo court. He (the youth) was trying to rob me, and we were scuffling, and I reached up on a shelf where I had a gun and I killed him with it. I shot him in self-defense. If I hadn't shot him, he would have killed me. It was him or me."

The Parole Board was not impressed by my argument that Leath's case deserved a more thorough investigation. I was heartened when I read on the AP wire that one of Leath's prosecutors had resigned because, according to the story, his "conscience troubled him" over the case. But the Parole Board was unyielding.

Leath trembled so violently that the prison barber could hardly shave his head for the electrode. Guards had to half-carry him to the Death House. At first he cringed when placed in the chair, then he slumped back as if retreating from everything. I suspect he was in a coma when the executioner hit the switch.

Like thousands of men before him, Leath was executed for reasons having no central bearing on the crime he was charged with committing, in my opinion. In the early 1960s, when he was tried and executed, he was "an odious thing" because of his homosexuality. A jury of the mid-1970s, even in Texas, might very well look upon his sexual aberration with some understanding and judge his degree of guilt strictly on the pertinent facts.

There was no way I could have helped Felix Adair, a white rapist, and two black rapists who died right behind him on the same night in what the Death Row wags called a "triple bill." The blacks, Allen Matthews and L.C. Simms, were guilty and had been fairly tried, as far as I could determine. Their blackness sealed their doom.

And Adair wanted to die. Indeed, he could hardly wait for death. He had staged what police called a series of "love burglaries" before he attacked a determined woman who fought him off and helped convict him. He was 27, a successful Dallas insurance man with a wife and family before he "went off the deep end" for a few weeks.

His behavior appeared so irrational for the steady, career-minded man his friends accepted that Adair was at first declared insane and committed to a state mental hospital. A year later he was prounced sane. He stood trial for rape and was given the death sentence.

From his sanity hearing to his moment of death Adair insisted he wanted to die. On his execution day he told me, "Don, I'm so relieved the end is in sight. I would rather die right now, be dead right now, than have my sentence commuted and have to go out and live in the prison yard the rest of my life with the black sin of guilt on my conscience." His voice carried such a ringing quality of truth that I winced and looked away from him.

He strode toward the little green door like a moth zeroing in on a candle, his eyes shining in anticipation. He smiled a "goodbye" to me as the guards lashed him to the chair. He died without a whimper.

Matthews and Simms followed him to the chair and, like Adair, went down without a word. I was weary when I finished dictating to Dallas the story of the "triple bill." We are all victims, I wanted to write but didn't. We say things in our daily, competitive lives we don't want to say, we do things we don't want to do, we deliver and receive wounds we truly don't want to exchange . . . and none of us emerges without sin.

At home later, musing over what I had witnessed, I recalled the hogwash spouted at the Austin hearing. In particular I remembered the witness who testified about the "racial proportions" of those executed. He had said the score was "about equally divided."

At the time of the hearing, 340 men had died in the electric chair . . . 216 blacks, 101 whites, 23 Mexican-Americans. About seventy percent of the state population was white, about fifteen percent was black, about fifteen percent Mexican-American. Of the executed men 63 percent were black, thirty percent white, seven percent Mexican-American.

Exactly 100 of the men were executed on charges of rape. And 75 were black, twenty were white and five were Mexican-American. "About equally divided," the witness had said.

W alter Whitaker was a rare bird on Death Row. He was white, young, rich and well-educated. He also was spoiled. Where Felix Adair had wanted to die, Whitaker simply did not care to live. He refused to cooperate with the excellent attorneys his wealthy Connecticut family hired to defend him. The only statement he made in court was one to the jury: "Well, I did it . . . what are you going to do about it?"

"It" was the murder of a beautiful young girl while they were eloping across West Texas.

Whitaker was in the U.S. Air Force. While stationed in West Texas he met the girl and wooed her. He received orders transferring him to San Antonio. The young couple decided to marry en route to his new station—and the girl did not tell her parents she was leaving home. She was reported "missing," and Texas Rangers began hunting her.

Rangers soon learned she had been "going steady" with Whitaker. They located him in San Antonio. Whitaker appeared puzzled. He had told the girl goodbye in Lubbock, he said. Rangers gave him a lie detector test. He "passed" the test so convincingly that the Rangers let him go with them to West Texas to search for the girl.

The girl could not be found. Grasping for clues, the Rangers asked Whitaker to submit to another lie detector test. He agreed—and passed with flying colors. But as the experts were removing their paraphernalia from Whitaker's body, the youth blurted out: "Oh, get these things off me and I'll tell you about it."

He took the Rangers to a spot where he had buried the girl's nude body in the backfill of a newly installed pump on an oil pipeline.

During his trial Whitaker refused to talk with anyone, even his lawyer. On Death Row he spurned newsmen, but every time I passed his cell I spoke to him. And one day he answered me with a "good morning" of his own. I said, "My son has the same first name you have. His name is Walter Reid."

Whitaker raised a brow. "Oh?"

He was 22, but with that raised eyebrow he looked like a kid trying to act grownup. Poor girl, I thought. Poor Walter. God have mercy on us all.

Whitaker began talking, anticipating my questions, pouring out thoughts and emotions he had confined in his mind and heart. For the first time on Death Row I was listening to a condemned man who really knew something of himself, who had probed his mind and conscience and examined them for flaws. Whitaker had an IQ of 135, and the prison psychiatrist could not have revealed the working of the youth's mind as well as Whitaker did that morning in his Death Row cell.

Whitaker knew he had been spoiled rotten. On one birthday, he said, his parents gave him a country estate. He shook his head. "They had to give me something impressive, I guess, because they were gone on tours so much of the time and it was a way of demonstrating that they really loved me." He raised that quizzical brow. "Now I know I really never felt their love for me, or mine for them."

Whitaker spoke precisely and enunciated clearly, and when I mentioned this he let me know he could speak Greek, Hebrew and all of the Romance languages. Laughing, he gave me a demonstration.

His laughter faded when I asked him about the girl. He said he hadn't intended to take the girl with him to San Antonio, that he had planned to send for her and marry her in the Alamo city. "But the night I was leaving she told me she was pregnant," he said, and his eyes lighted up as he recalled the moment. "She said she knew we were going to have a boy, and it was the greatest thrill I had ever felt. That's when we decided to elope."

Riding along the deserted highway in the night, the couple decided to park off the highway and make love to celebrate their happiness, the unborn child and their coming marriage, Whitaker said.

After their lovemaking, as they held each other and talked of the future, the girl confessed that she was not pregnant, Whitaker said. She never had time to explain why she had lied.

Now Whitaker was pacing his cell. "I went absolutely berserk. She was taking something away from me that was mine. Something I had created." He looked at me intently. He was breathing heavily. "That baby she lied about was something of my own I was responsible for, not something someone had given me." He turned his back on me and I could hear the air hiss through his teeth. "I guess I just beat her to death."

Long moments passed. I saw his head tilt forward as he stared at the cell floor. He began talking, and because his back was to me I had to strain to hear him. "Maybe she was just testing my love," he said. "She was as young and ignorant as I was. Maybe that's why she did it." A pause. "Maybe she wanted to give me an 'out.' Perhaps she was going to say, 'Since I'm not pregnant, Walter, you don't have to marry me if you don't want to.'" A pause. "Perhaps she just reasoned that a quick marriage based on a lie couldn't be a good one." He shook his head. "I don't know, Mr. Reid, I don't know."

He turned around. His eyes were wet, but a wry grin was on his lips. "You see, I was a spoiled boy and the one I loved had 'let me down,' as they used to say. So I messed up everything."

The grin went away. He surveyed me coolly. His voice was distant as he said, "I messed up everything, and there's very little I want to do about it now." He turned from me. I was dismissed. Walter Whitaker had retreated into his protective shell.

But I had to have the answer to one question. I said, "Why did you suddenly confess after you had beaten the lie detector twice?"

He turned to face me, shaking his head as he did so. I can't explain it," he said, "but I'll tell you what I think. I think it was because my mind was clearing up, because it was throwing off the shock of the whole, terrible experience."

"Tell me . . . ."

But Whitaker turned away again.

On his execution night he prayed briefly in his cell with a Lutheran minister, then walked to his death without a word to anyone.

At the Austin hearing the Reverend Robert Ingram of Houston had called for "an eye for an eye," and I suppose he would have approved of Whitaker's execution as suitable retribution for his crime. I thought at the time, and I think now, that Walter Whitaker, at 22, was worth trying to help. I believe that proper psychiatric treatment could have helped make him a stable citizen. And Walter Whitaker as a stable citizen could have made a contribution to the lives of others.

Felix Adair wanted to die; Walter Whitaker didn't care to live. But Howard Stickney fought for his life through thirteen stays of execution in a succession of legal maneuvers that consumed four years and twice snatched him from the Death Chamber even as the executioner sat fingering his controls.

Stickney was a twenty-year-old soil technician for the state when he was charged with the murder of a young couple named Clifford and Shirley Barnes. At fifteen he had been arrested as a window peeper, and the slayings had just such sexual overtones. Shirley Barnes' nude and beaten body was found on a bed in her Houston apartment. Later police found Barnes' body under a pile of brush in the Brazos River bottoms west of the city. Further investigations showed that the couple and Stickney had been at a beach party in Galveston shortly before Shirley Barnes' body was found.

Stickney eluded police until he was captured in Canada by Mounties as he sought to book passage to Europe. He was tried in Houston, convicted and given the death sentence.

Stickney had talents I'm sure he hadn't known he possessed. He was bright and handsome. He learned quickly, and he discovered that he could be as glib and articulate as a television master of ceremonies. Within weeks after he reached Death Row he was operating as a master publicist. No U.S. President ever manipulated the news media more cleverly than Stickney. He learned the news deadlines of every major newspaper and radio station in the state. He milked newspaper readers and radio listeners for sympathy and support with such success that university students marched about their campuses in protest of his sentence. Students advanced on the governor's office in Austin with petitions demanding that Stickney's life be spared. And this, mind you, was in a time before students were activists—and in a state where student protests were seldom heard even later when they became the order of the day elsewhere.

Newsmen from the state's major cities and from other states as well trooped to Stickney's cell almost daily. For each he had a plum, a fresh and lively quote to sustain the controversy that swirled around his conviction. And all the while his attorneys were busy with briefs in courtrooms both state and federal.

It would not be exaggerating to say that Stickney managed to keep much of the state in an uproar. At one point he had a sober district judge and a fiery district attorney shouting at each other in headlines of shocking virulence. Judge Cullen Briggs of Corpus Christi—who had not presided at Stickney's trial—dealt Stickney a reprieve at the very moment Stickney was rubbing his hand across the shaved spot on his skull and waiting for the warden to invite him to "have a seat."

The reprieve so infuriated Houston District Attorney Frank Briscoe that he stormed out of a Texas Bar Association convention in Fort Worth demanding that the Texas Court of Criminal Appeals throw the book at Judge Briggs. Newsmen were delighted. Judge Briggs countered with a four-page "finding of fact" that disputed the state's handling of the case on practically all points. And the finding flatly said that Dan Walton, Briscoe's predecessor and Stickney's prosecutor, had suppressed evidence and testimony which could have greatly illuminated the issue of Stickney's guilt or innocence. The Court of Criminal Appeals promptly told Judge Briggs to stop interfering in the case.

The complete truth about the Stickney-Barnes case probably never will be revealed. No one ever admitted witnessing the two killings, and the evidence mounted against Stickney at his trial was circumstantial and, in the eyes of many, incomplete.

Stickney was tried for the slaying of Shirley Barnes. He was convicted on the basis of circumstantial evidence and a confession which he later repudiated and which was considerably mangled by the state's own witnesses at the trial.

The confession to police was made orally first to C.A. (Red) Dwyer, the Harris County health officer who doubled as county psychiatrist in criminal matters. Dwyer was a warm and friendly man whose chief virtues were a firm belief in the value of friendship and a staunch devotion to those whom he befriended. No one ever called him a great doctor. If he ever testified in variance to the state's contention as to a man's sanity, I can't recall the case. "Red" was a DA's man.

Dwyer testified that Stickney told him he had been window-peeping at Shirley Barnes and had been masturbating while watching her use the bathroom. He had fallen in love with her. Dwyer felt that Stickney didn't like Clifford

Barnes' treatment of Shirley. Dwyer said he thought Clifford Barnes had suggested going to Galveston beach to pick up some girls, Shirley did not approve of the suggestion, and Stickney interceded in her behalf. "He didn't want to see the woman he loved treated in such a way by her own husband," Dwyer said.

They all three went to Galveston, Dwyer continued. Barnes and Stickney slept on a blanket by the car while Shirley stayed in the car from fear of snakes. The night grew cool and Stickney went to the car trunk to get an extra blanket. He saw a tire tool and brought it back and hit Barnes once or twice. Shirley was alarmed and said she'd tell on him, so he hit her, too, and then held her head under water until she couldn't breathe. He stripped her and washed the blood off her. Later, while he was carrying her into her apartment, he was aroused sexually and, having placed a pillow over her head, took her.

Other prosecution witnesses said that evidence taken from Stickney's car showed that a bleeding body or bodies had been carried in it. It was established that Shirley had been taken sexually. A chemist testified that two hairs lifted from seminal stains on the bed had "identical characteristics" with those of Stickney's pubic hair and probably were Stickney's.

But the county medical officer who conducted an autopsy testified that there was no saltwater in Shirley's nasal passages and stomach, and that the water would have been there had Stickney held Shirley under water until she could not breathe. He also said he found no sand or signs of beachcombing on her body, and that dirt on the soles of her feet was not beach sand but the kind of dirt she would have picked up from a linoleum floor in an apartment.

And he also testified that from the amount of blood on the bed he concluded that Shirley was still living when she lay down on the bed or was placed there. The blood could not have flowed from her had she not had a living circulatory system at the time.

Stickney did not testify. After the trial he said he confessed because he was promised psychiatric care if he did so—that he was told to make his story so fantastic and gruesome no one would believe it and the psychiatric care would follow.

Dwyer said only that he told Stickney he would transmit his request for the care to the proper authorities, and did tell District Attorney Walton about it. It was reported, but not confirmed, that Dwyer was upset because Stickney was not released from jail long enough to undergo a complete mental examination before the trial.

But it was what occurred after the trial that created so much turmoil. Several people came forward with stories that might have proved helpful to Stickney at the trial. Among them were a Houston oil company employee, his brother-in-law and their young sons. They said they had seen the Barnes-Stickney group on the beach in the afternoon, and later in the evening stopped at the scene because Stickney was unconscious on the ground with a lump on his head while Barnes and another man, James Vittitoe, were threatening each other with tire tools. The argument apparently had arisen because Barnes had asked Shirley to strip, thus angering both Stickney and Vittitoe. The oil company employee, R.E.L. Fox, said he shared Vittitoe's indignation, and that they exchanged identification notes so Fox could be a witness for Vittitoe if it ever became necessary. Stickney was still unconscious when he left the scene, he said. Fox said he told the district attorney's office what he had seen but was never called to testify.

Stickney had never mentioned a James Vittitoe in his statements to police, but he had casually mentioned a "Jim V." to his attorneys at various times—so casually, in fact, that no one had questioned him further.

James Vittitoe was located. He denied being at the beach or knowing the Barnes couple. But he did admit that Stickney came to him after the slaying and said he needed money for a trip. He said he gave Stickney about $100. Later he declared that Stickney told him about the killings and asked for money to get to Canada. Police said he took a lie detector test which proved he was not on the beach, and that Fox failed to pick Vittitoe out of a special police lineup. Then Fox's brother-in-law, Herman Anderson, repudiated his story. Others who had stories to tell repudiated theirs. A federal judge ruled at a subsequent hearing that Fox's story was fantastic and false, but at a hearing before Judge Briggs, Anderson's son corroborated the Fox account, which Anderson had verified and then repudiated. It was from this hearing that Judge Briggs derived his "finding of fact" that the state had concealed and suppressed evidence. He listed other persons, who had told stories and repudiated them, whose presence at a trial he considered vital.

The case see-sawed back and forth over the years until at last the U. S. Supreme Court and several other lesser courts all refused to hear anymore about it. Stickney was stuck, as one newspaper headline put it.

During all this time Stickney talked about almost everything in the world except his guilt or innocence. Certainly he knew something about the slayings. But on Death Row Stickney maintained that he could remember nothing about the fatal night, and he talked occasionally of a concussion—an implication that he was struck on the head by Clifford Barnes and so suffered a blackout. (Fox had said he saw Stickney on the ground, unconscious and with a lump on his head.)

I watched Stickney mature on Death Row. I also saw him take the "Jesus Route" each time his string began running out. I became convinced that as a child he had been punished severely for some sexual wrong and suffered from the experience thereafter. I believe this occurred some years before he was "arrested" as a window-peeper at the age of fifteen. There was something wrong with Stickney mentally, a vague "something" I would sense from time to time, and I'm sure it resulted from those traumas of his youth. Stickney's ego would not permit him to admit it, but I know he felt that he was "not quite right" to some degree.

Stickney didn't need my help and never asked for it. Dozens of reporters more skilled at investigative work than I had combed through "clues" and "evidence" for months.

So had lawyers. But we talked often, and he appeared to trust me. More, he seemed to have a little more regard for me than he had for other newsmen whom he sometimes referred to as "my press agents."

Once I gave him a list of questions he said he would answer in writing but not orally. His replies were vague and quite uncommunicative:

Q: Who do you believe killed Shirley and Clifford Barnes?

A: Being judged myself, I couldn't judge so offhandedly.

Q: As nearly as you can remember, what happened that night on the Galveston beach?

A: Again, I wish I had the time.

Q: If you are granted another trial, will you insist on taking the witness stand?

A. I would want to, but circumstances are only guessable.

Q: Why did you flee to Canada after Shirley and Clifford were killed?

A: I was advised to by Jim V. and was too young and shook up to have sense.

Q: If you awakened today and found the bodies of Shirley and Clifford beside you, what would you do differently?

A: Call the police, and the following is easy to see.

Q: Have you withheld evidence (which would have involved others) that could have cleared you?

A. Not to my knowledge, although we have not publicly made it all known as it would only have helped before a jury.

Q: Who really killed Shirley and Clifford Barnes?

A: I wouldn't be here if I knew that.

Q: Tell me anything you remember of that night.

A: I wish I had the time and space to answer.

Q: Was evidence suppressed that could have cleared you?

A: That would be an opinion, but what we have taken

into hearing, if before a jury, wouldn't have me here writing this tonight.

Later on he handed me a thick sheaf of handwritten pages. His execution date was only a few weeks away. He asked me not to make the papers public until after his death. "I don't want it to appear like I'm hunting public sympathy," he said.

I could hardly restrain a smile. For more than three years he had fought for and garnered more public sympathy than any other Death Row inmate could have dreamed about. But I agreed to his request.

And Stickney got another reprieve. A few days later he asked me if I would go ahead and make the statement public. "Not for me, Don," he said, "but because it may help others who are waiting for execution." I said I would.

He had labeled the statement "The Law of Dis-Association." I have no idea how many newspapers ran parts of it, but some ran the piece in its entirety. It went like this:

> Today and every day I must sit here and accept the fact that like it or not, my friends, attorneys and even family will, with all the people of Texas, have a hand, reluctant or not, upon the switch when next it is pulled. This is a very depressing thought for me, but how do you feel? Did you know your hand was there? Had you ever thought of it? This is why I am writing this, to make you think and in thinking, hope you will do something towards removing your hand. Would you wish for someone to sign checks in your name all over the state? Of course not, for it could ruin your name or credit.
>
> By the same token would you wish for a person's life to be taken in your name, and his life upon your conscience? Every time a person is executed, that is what happens.
>
> What of a man from El Paso who was out-of-state from January through March, and in that time a crime was committed in Port Arthur, a man tried

and convicted, and a sentence of death carried out? Is the El Paso man still responsible in any way, for the poor man had no knowledge of any of it? In answer, all that can be done is ask, is he a citizen of Texas? Then it is his law and was carried out in his name.

But you say you were not on the jury? Just because you did not vote for the governor, does that make him any less your governor? The law which enables the death penalty to exist, which I call the law of disassociation, is meant to either protect or punish you, as the case may be. It is your law, brought into being in your name and signed in to law by your officials.

The juries which assess the death penalty as a punishment do so in your name, and the order of execution says . . . "the people of the State of Texas . . . ," giving your name to even this final act. So whom—and the responsibility must be acknowledged —bears this taking of life upon their conscience? The governor for signing it into law? The DA for asking it? The jury for giving it? The executioner for carrying it out? Just as the law is yours, these acts are carried out in your name and it is upon your conscience that the life or lives taken must be placed.

Give it time to sink in. Had you ever realized it was so? Did you know that from July, 1960, to April, 1961, five men were put to death in your name? Did you even know their names, let alone why? Did you really care or pay any attention? Or did you disassociate yourself? Again we come to this.

The reason I call it "The Law of Dis-Association" is because I feel and believe that it could not exist year after year as a law if everyone did associate themselves. Have you ever followed a case and at its close been dissatisfied, saying, "I sure was sorry to see that, but I wasn't on the jury and had no part of it?" That is disassociation.

If you believe in the death penalty, but do not or

will not accept the responsibility of EVERY LIFE TAKEN within your own conscience, that is disassociation. If you believe in it and accept the responsibility, I can only say this to you:

Would you want God, not knowing the facts but taking the opinion of 12 others you don't know, to condemn you so readily? I say it that way because you, the average Texan, could not know every fact in every case where death is assessed, a death which you so readily accept in your conscience.

If you believe in the death penalty in some cases, but not in others, you are in effect saying, "I'm letting all these juries give death penalties to all these people that I don't feel should be put to death, but I'm letting them do it in my name and am willing to accept the conscientious responsibility for these because one may come along that I'd feel should be put to death."

If, of four men given the death penalty, you felt two deserved it and two didn't, by your own feelings the two UNdeserving would be put to death NOT for their crimes, but for the crimes of the other. Had you thought of that?

By having a death penalty, whenever you feel it unjust, you are punishing that person not for what they did, but for the crime for which you reserve the death penalty to be a just punishment.

Could you feel one sentence unjust, stand by and let it be carried out, and then be able to look the parents, wife, or children of that person in the eye? Change places with them for a moment and see how you like yourself. This is no joking matter. It's a matter of human life, just like your own, your parents, your children.

Think of the difference in your own mind, of the years in prison and eventual parole compared to the finality of death for yourself or a loved one. You don't believe it could happen to you or them? Ask any man on Death Row or his family if they believed it could happen. Ask the families of the inmates in our prison system!

But the remoteness of it happening to you is not the point I'm trying to stress, but the injustice of disassociation, allowing it to happen.

Lastly, if you do not believe in the death penalty, but do nothing, you are disassociating yourself in the worst way.

You, of all people, have done the condemned man the most injustice by denying him. Please, don't you know that belief in God and Jesus is not enough by itself, that you have to do something about it and ask forgiveness to be saved?

If you saw a child stranded in the middle of a busy intersection and knew that to leave him there without help would mean his death, would you know this and do nothing?

A man who is caught up in the complexity of law and courts and writs and procedure is no more than a child. But you say his life will be guarded by his own attorneys or the state will furnish his attorneys?

Those drivers out there are licensed and their automobiles inspected for proficiency in such a situation, but not every driver has the means or ability to react to such a situation.

Have you faced one like it? Not every attorney has the means to protect their client, for not all have handled a like situation or gone before the different appeal courts. If you would not leave it all to the driver's ability, then you should not leave it all to the attorney's.

But you still say it isn't a good example because the child in all innocence probably wandered into the street, and the person is probably guilty to some degree, for a jury found him so?

Now you are again hunting for an out, wanting again the anonymity of disassociation, and I'll show you why, for two reasons.

It is not guilt, but the degree of that guilt that

determines, or should determine, what punishment a jury assesses. Not believing in the death penalty, then to you no such degree of guilt could exist!

Secondly, if you can think of no conceivable way the child could have arrived at his or her present predicament that would merit death, then you, not believing in a penalty of death, should not find a conceivable act or crime that should merit death. It is not how they got there that counts when a life is at stake, but the fact that life will be taken if someone does not act.

Death by an automobile or death in the electric chair, one horrible to the imagination and the other said to be painless by experts who have never tried it themselves, is not the question either. It is not how, but the very thing of death itself. Which would be more important to you—how you died or whether you lived or died?

Now, on the argument that the death penalty is a deterrent to crime. The word "deter" means restrain, discourage, prevent, hold back, or withhold by fear. In other words, then, the argument is that the death penalty will discourage, withhold by fear, or restrain people from committing crimes which are punishable by that penalty.

That does not mean prevent when they are caught, or restrain them when they are before a jury, but restrain or hold them by fear from the act of commission of a crime punishable by death.

At the commission is when the possibility of a death penalty is supposed to deter or refrain people then.

Let me ask you this: How many crimes have been committed since death has been a punishment, where that crime at the commission could have been punishable by death?

If the law says that crime is punishable by death, a person committing it has no way at the commission to know what punishment a jury will give him if he is caught. All he could know is he could be put to death but he may not even know that.

Do YOU know every set of circumstances where the law says the death penalty can be asked?

Do YOU think every person knows at the time, if he even thinks, that what he is doing could be punishable by death? Where is the great deterrent power?

Take two crimes, one not so horrible, like a midnight burglary, and the other, a horrible premeditated murder. The law says death can be a punishment in both of those crimes, but it did not deter either person even though they knew this.

The one who committed murder has the money to hire a good attorney and finance the paperwork and research needed, but the burglar has no money and so must depend on a state-appointed attorney who, if he can do even the simple research needed to defend his pauper client, must do it on his own and at his own expense.

Can you see what could happen at those trials? But that could happen in any case or crime, you say? People, we aren't talking of one or two or five years of a man's life, we are talking of his life itself.

So where has the death penalty deterred, or where is it good when the circumstances of his friends, family, position in life, or the competence of his attorney so bear upon his eventual punishment at his trial, for these make mockery of the argument of determent at the commission of a crime or trial upon the merits of that crime alone.

If this were true, and they could be, would you want that person's life on your conscience for stealing at night from a home, when you knew that the man who committed a premeditated murder was alive in prison and might someday be paroled back into your society?

I'm asking that regardless of how you feel on the death penalty, for it could happen as long as there is a death penalty.

As long as there is a death penalty, the lives taken are taken in your name, and regardless of your own feelings, are upon your conscience.

If you are only one year over voting age, then there are more lives on your conscience now than were known to be on any one person's conscience who has been put to death in Texas in the electric chair.

That's right now. How many more will you add. And to you who are under the voting age to do anything about it now, look at the legacy awaiting you. All I want to know is, how can you sleep tonight?

What can you do about it? Express yourself instead of disassociating yourself. Have your friends read this. How many do you have? 10? 20? 50? 700? Did you ever stop to think that each of them has as many friends, and that with only 10 friends apiece, you and 10 friends know 100 people.

With all this starting with you alone, you have a block of votes and voices already. Can you see how it could multiply? Won't you do something? Won't you see if you cannot only take your hand off the switch and save these lives from your conscience, but do away completely with a switch or any of its counterparts entirely?

Because since you do not know why in every case, your only answer to your conscience now for these lives, or eventually, to God, is that they were taken for "something or another." If this is your only answer, may God have more mercy upon you than you have had upon others!

Publication of the article created another furor around the state. It and Stickney were denounced in some quarters. In others there were clamors for commutation of his sentence. It would be fair to say Stickney enjoyed it all. Yet, the statement was one of the few sober expressions he had made on Death Row, one not tinged with press-agentry.

There was a hint of anger in it, it seemed to me, as if he were saying, "Damn it, this is the way I *really* feel."

If his hopes ever flagged, I was never able to detect it.

But there came the day when I went to his cell with Chaplain J.N. Foreman to tell him that the U.S. Supreme Court, four other federal courts and several state courts had all refused to consider his case further.

Stickney took a deep drag on his cigarette and carefully ground it out on an ashtray. He mustered a smile. "Well," he said, "I gave 'em a run for their money, didn't I?" He had accepted that he would die. And with that acceptance he immediately took steps to insure as far as possible that his travels on the "Jesus Route" would be rewarding. Three chaplains were with him during his final hours, and on his cot were three different Bibles. Over and over he read the 23rd Psalm. Once when I walked by his cell he stopped me. He put a hand through the bars and placed it on my shoulder. "You sure look tired, Don," he said. "Don't overdo yourself." He squeezed my shoulder and returned to his reading.

Stickney had said all he could say or wanted to say when the time came for him to die. He went to the chair silently and died without a murmur.

I think Stickney killed Clifford and Shirley Barnes. I'm convinced he was mentally ill. He was only 24 when he died. It would have taken a long period of treatment to have "cured" him, but his youth was in his favor. It would have been "worth" the time and effort.

At the Austin hearing I had hoped to explore the practice of separately trying two or more suspects in the same crime. Quite often a man would receive the death penalty while his partner, tried at a different time before a different jury, would be sentenced to life imprisonment. Whether a man lived or died in those instances quite obviously depended primarily on the skill of his defender and the quality of the prosecution. It was grossly unfair . . . from the point of view of the one who received the death sentence.

And I also had hoped for wide-open discussion of confessions taken by force. Every police reporter worth his salt knows that police brutality is far from being as rare as police and prosecutors would have the public believe. Most police reporters, however, close their eyes to the practice or grow to accept it much in the same way rookie policemen grow to accept it. Many police reporters, to their detriment, simply develop the police mentality or, as some city editors describe it, "get a cophouse complex." Around a police station or courthouse a reporter who is "defense-minded" oftentimes has to scramble for news other reporters are handed freely. A reporter may handle police news objectively, but he cannot cover a police beat for long and maintain an objective personal attitude.

Neither issue was discussed in Austin. I had wanted to introduce the case of Darius Goleman and Alec Leviness. They were charged with the murder of Eloise Twitchell, an East Texas school teacher. The state said the men were given a ride by the woman as they hitchhiked through the "Big Thicket" area of East Texas.

Leviness was given life. Another jury handed Goleman the death sentence.

Goleman was the most bitter man I saw on Death Row. He hated newsmen of all stripes. He had refused to talk with any reporter from the time his arrest was announced until the day before his execution. All that I had learned about him was that he had previously served a term for robbery . . . and that he and Leviness had been arrested by Ranger John Klevenhagen and Harris County Sheriff Buster Kern, the "Gold Dust Twins."

On the day before his execution he asked his jailers to summon me to Death Row. This man had brushed aside friendly overtures by chaplains and guards, and I was surprised that he wanted to see me.

He was thirty—hazel-eyed, dark-haired, slight of build. A Houston reporter had described him as "an ex-convict from Goose Creek who was named for a Persian king . . . ." There was nothing majestic about Goleman save his anger. He was in a towering rage, as if he had spent every moment on Death Row stoking the fire of his bitterness and had now built up a suitable head of steam.

He came on strong, with no amenities. "I'm breaking my word to myself, but I decided I want to get my story printed. Can you do it?"

"Maybe," I ventured.

"Maybe, hell! I know it won't do no good, you understand. It won't help me any. But by God I'm not gonna let these people kill me without having a say. I've made up my mind, you understand?"

"Say your say," I told him.

"I didn't kill that woman and those bastards know I didn't kill her. They beat that confession out of me and I tell you, by God, no man can stand up under that kind of treatment. I'd have told 'em I helped crucify Christ if they had wanted me to. I held out a long time, you understand. Those bastards shifted me around from county to county so no lawyer could get to me. One sheriff, the one in Hardin County, told me he'd hang me in his jail and tell the newspapers I had committed suicide unless I signed a statement. That's the kind of stuff I mean. That and beating hell out of a man, beating him and beating him until he can't hold out. Sure I confessed. Maybe it makes me less than a man in your eyes, but you ain't ever been handled that way . . ."

I interrupted him. "If you weren't in on the killing, where were you when it happened?"

"I was in Houston. I was with some of my relatives. But hell, nobody believes an ex-convict and nobody believes relatives of ex-convicts and my relatives had police records, too. My record makes anything I say a God damned lie, don't you know that? And I had a brother, they called him 'Red' Goleman. He was a bank robber, and he got killed in a shootout just outside Liberty, and by God, that's where they tried me . . . in a place where everybody remembered my brother."

Suddenly he shook his head wearily. "Ah, bullshit!" He stepped back and sat down on his cot. He looked at the floor. "How about coming back tomorrow and eating with me?" he asked. "Can you do it?"

"I'll be here," I told him.

I was back the next day. Goleman was no gourmet. We

ate tamales, crackers, cookies and ice cream as we faced each other through the cell bars. I had been told no chaplain had been to see Goleman on this day, and I asked him why. He said grimly, "There ain't no forgiveness in me. I can't make myself forget Kern and Klevenhagen and those others. To hell with this crap about forgiving somebody who wants you dead for something you didn't do." He looked at me defiantly. "I'll feel the same way when I go through the little green door, and you'd better believe it."

At midnight Goleman strode swiftly and silently through the little green door and to the waiting chair. He ignored the warden and the guards. And as the guards were lashing him to "Old Sparky" he said in a loud, clear voice, "I'm innocent. I didn't kill Eloise Twitchell."

If he wanted to say more it was cut off by the surge of electricity through his body. In minutes "the word" was flashing through the prison that Goleman had "died game."

Darius Goleman was not a lovely person. Perhaps he was an evil man. Perhaps he went to his death with a lie on his lips. But he should not have died while Alec Leviness lived on.

And I could not dismiss completely his story of being beaten by Kern and Klevenhagen. The public respected the two lawmen. Indeed, for a long while they were almost idolized for their ability to quickly solve crimes and obtain confessions. But Louis Marino, for one, obviously was badly mistreated while in their hands. And their violent natures flared through when they attacked the crippled Percy Foreman after he won freedom for Diego Carlino, who also claimed his confession was forced from him.

9

The Law and
Joe Edward Smith

We had the facts and figures. Each charter member of
the Texas Society to Abolish Capital Punishment had gathered stacks of facts and figures. I combed the Uniform
Crime Reports of the FBI, drew from the archives of the
National Council on Crime and Delinquency, studied bulle-
tins from the Federal Bureau of Prisons, pored over pages of
the Congressional Record. Time and again I went through
the files of the Texas Department of Corrections and devoured studies prepared by the highly regarded Department
of Sociology of Texas Southern University in Houston. And,
of course, I had right at hand the Death Row files—and the
inmates themselves.

We had promised ourselves we would be well prepared
to do battle at the next capital punishment hearing in Austin.
So well prepared, in fact, that we could take our message to
the people with speeches and through the news media even
before the hearing began.

My approach was not scientific, I'm sure. When I found
something of value I would put it in a file under an appropriate heading. When a particular folder began to bulge, I
would take off an evening or a Saturday or Sunday and go
to my office to assemble the material into a manageable and
workable tool. On one such occasion I heard Frances tell
a friend over the telephone, "Don's going to the office to
draft some more troops."

I had an army, but I finally whittled it down to a platoon. I settled on the statistics that I reasoned listeners could easily understand. I hoped they would agree with the conclusions the statistics so clearly established.

The most telling figures—and the ones easiest to grasp —were in a comparison of the number of murders per 100,000 population in capital punishment states with the number of murders per 100,000 population in states where life imprisonment was the maximum penalty. To reduce arguments, I chose a year in the late 1950s as the proper period to make the comparisons—a time between the Korean War and the war in Southeast Asia, a time of relative peace for the U.S. and a time when the economy was reasonably stable.

Of the life imprisonment states, Michigan was nearest Texas in population. In the key year there were 4.1 murders per 100,000 population in Michigan. In Texas there were 10.6.

The figures, of course, did not take into account a population's racial makeup, its heritage, its skills, its educational level. But Texans' virtues were not so few and their faults so many that the state should have more than twice as many killings as Michigan. If we could not credit Michigan's low murder rate to its life imprisonment policy, we certainly could not argue that Texas' capital punishment policy had accomplished anything at all. And the two-to-one ratio had held fairly steady for decades before the key year, and it held fairly steady in after years.

The Michigan-Texas comparative figures were a pattern. Wisconsin's rate with life imprisonment was 1.7, compared with Georgia's 13.9. Minnesota's rate was 1.0, compared with Alabama's 16.2. Maine's rate was 1.2, compared with Colorado's 3.9. Rhode Island's rate was 1.2, compared with Arizona's 13.9. And so it went.

This argument did not appear specious to my listeners, and it wasn't. After a speech in which I would dwell on many points, invariably a member of the audience would rise and ask, "Mr. Reid, are you telling us that people do more killing in states where they have the chair or whatever than in states where they don't?" The questioner's voice most often held wonderment, not skepticism, and the hostility I had encountered in the past was absent.

"Yes," I would say, "I'm telling you just that. I think you know I wouldn't lie about something that important. But the simple truth is that murder and rape go on in every state, and the threat of the chair doesn't stop them. It never has. It never will. The threat of life imprisonment doesn't stop them, either, but it does as good a job, or better, than the threat of the chair." I would pause, but before my questioner could quite sit down, I would add, "If you happen to kill an innocent man in the chair, you've done a terrible thing. If you happen to give an innocent man life imprisonment, you've got a chance to right a wrong. That's worth thinking about, isn't it?"

My listeners were still not interested in the harsh inequities of the administration of justice as far as capital punishment was concerned. They still withdrew somewhat when I pointed out the obvious racial discrimination, the social discrimination. They were not impressed that 3,859 persons had been executed in the U.S. since 1930 without being slowed perceptibly. They apparently already assumed that of the 460 men who had sat on Texas' Death Row by this time the great majority were uneducated—that only fourteen percent of the blacks, 25 percent of the whites and four percent of the Mexicans had ever seen the inside of a high school . . . that only two blacks and six whites had ever attended college; that fifty percent of the blacks and Mexican-Americans and a third of the whites had no occupational skills at all, and only 26—six blacks and twenty whites— could be considered having been in an upper occupation scale.

Perhaps I was too dogged, but I crammed them full of statistics and "for instances." So did my colleagues around the state. We pounded home some views that the U.S. Supreme Court and other courts later considered and agreed with. That is not to boast. More capable men than we were doing their fighting in other arenas, and it was their untiring efforts that wrought the changes.

Texans like to believe they are a fair-minded people, and generally they are. I used that belief when I would point out that jury selection in a capital case was patently unfair. "Every one of you knows," I would say, "that the DA questions every prospective juror closely on his belief in the death penalty. If the prospect says he doesn't favor the death penalty, or has doubts about its efficacy as a deterrent, the DA won't select him—even if he's the community's finest citizen. So the jury finally is composed of twelve folks who believe in the death penalty—and in a lot of cases are raring to hand it down. This doesn't make sense. A guy is supposed to be tried by a jury that is a representative of his community. None of you folks would want to play poker with the deck stacked against you, but that's what the DA is doing in capital cases. He's stacking the deck."

That made sense to many of them. I wasn't "taking up" for niggers and mescans and sorry whites. I was talking about what was fair and what was unfair.

"I'll tell you something else that's not fair," I would say. "During one ten-year period I studied, police said there were almost 18,000 homicides in Texas. Eighteen thousand! Out of that large number only 231 men got the death penalty. A lot of men got lesser penalties, but only 231 got the death penalty. Now, out of that 231, only 145 were electrocuted. 18,000 killings, and when the bingo game was over, everybody who had killed somebody got off with his life intact except 145 guys. Don't tell me that the other men were better people, or that their killings were a little bit more merciful. You know better than that. They were spared because they had better lawyers, or they knew people with influence, or they pleaded insanity and were believed. The United States Constitution prohibits cruel and unusual punishment. Don't tell me it's not cruel and unusual punishment when only a handful of guys get electrocuted and thousands who killed miss the chair. That's *darned* unusual punishment, and it's terribly cruel . . . ."

So, the only points I was able to drive home were three —that there were less or no more murders committed in life imprisonment states than in capital punishment states, that jury selection in capital cases was patently unfair, and that who was executed for murder and who wasn't was what one man called a "grisly lottery."

The same was true for my colleagues.

We felt we were making an impact in the hinterland, but the Austin hearing for which we had prepared did not come to pass. Other men in other areas were making a far greater impact in the courts across the country. Complaints about the maladministration of capital punishment were channeled through organizations with legal facilities, organizations interested in protecting the civil and legal rights of all American citizens.

One court decision after another, beginning in 1963, struck down practices that police and prosecutors had held inviolate for decades and decades. By 1965 so many appeals were before the courts that executions were braked shortly to just seven in the country. The decline started in 1962 with 47, dropped to 21 in 1963, to fifteen in 1964 and then seven in 1965. There was one execution in 1966, two in 1967. That ended it. The last one in Texas was in 1964. The moratorium was unofficial, of course. It was made official by the U.S. Supreme Court decision of June 29, 1972.

Leaders in the legal fight against capital punishment were lawyers for the National Association for the Advancement of Colored People and the American Civil Liberties Union. They hacked paths through the legal jungle to obtain clear-cut definitions of society's rights, including those of alleged criminals.

The Melvin Bellises, the F. Lee Baileys, the Percy Foremans, brilliant and successful as they may be, generally operated on a purely local or regional level, picking and choosing their cases. They built their cases around a superb knowledge of the law and the men who enforce and prosecute, an incisive understanding of local habits and mores, and an uncanny knowledge of people and the decisions they might render. They commanded—and needed—huge fees to finance their efforts.

The lawyers manning the battlements for the ACLU and the NAACP, and the occasional civil rights attorney making the fight on his own, operated from a different support base. Many were basically legal scholars and researchers. They sought and obtained financial grants and donations to keep their efforts going. Often they donated their time and talents, and finances, in behalf of the poor and ignorant.

Theirs was a grubby, time-consuming, exacting struggle over the years, far from the limelight of the courtroom, as they x-rayed the legal beams that held our judicial structure together. It was a sifting, sorting, exploring pursuit of a dream that, someday, they would strip aside the blubber of tradition and expose society's rights which were hidden away behind ancient biblical injunctions and paranoidal fears.

Their work bore fruit. Decisions of the U. S. Supreme Court—the so-called "Warren Court"—took a dramatic turn from the traditional renderings that had frustrated defense attorneys for so many years. The impact of these high court decisions, of course, reached down to courts of appeal and original jurisdiction.

New legal terminology began to appear in the country's newspapers: Mallory v. Hogan, Gideon v. Wainwright, Escabedo v. Illinois, People v. Morse, Miranda v. Arizona, Witherspoon v. Illinois, Jackson v. Denno.

Police and prosecutors cried out against the decisions. The high court, they said, was tying their hands; they could not control crime and punish offenders. Their concern was reflected on editorial pages.

This was nonsense. Mallory v. Hogan held that the Fourteenth Amendment guaranteed the same privilege against state invasion of rights that the Fifth Amendment guarantees—the right of a person to remain silent unless he chooses to speak and to suffer no penalty for such silence. Gideon v. Wainwright held that the right to counsel in federal courts, required by the Sixth Amendment, is extended to defendants in state prosecutions by the due process clause of the Fourteenth Amendment.

Escabedo v. Illinois held that a defendant's statements

made during the "pre-arraignment accusatory stage of an interrogation"—when police are trying to get a confession before filing charges—cannot be admitted into evidence if, at that stage, the defendant was denied the right to legal counsel.

People v. Morse held that a jury's function in determining the penalty for a crime is to consider the facts presented and the defendant's background. The jury should not be invited to consider any future release or weigh possible future parole board action. This was to stop prosecutors from saying to the jury, "If you give this man life, he'll get out on parole in ten years—and you don't want that, do you?"

Miranda v. Arizona held that the prosecution may not use statements stemming from "custodial interrogation" of the defendant unless it shows that safeguards were used to protect the defendant from self-incrimination. After a person has been taken into custody he must be warned that he has the right to remain silent, that any statement he makes may be used as evidence against him, and that he has the right to the presence of a lawyer. He may dispense with these rights, but if he indicates in any manner at any stage of the process that he wishes to consult a lawyer before speaking, questioning must cease until he obtains or is provided with an attorney.

Witherspoon v. Illinois was a California Supreme Court decision which reversed the death penalty given two men on grounds that prospective jurors had been improperly excused because of their opposition to the death penalty. By excluding veniremen who indicated they were opposed to the death penalty, the prosecution had selected a jury not representative of the community.

This new doctrine was retroactive—and attorneys across the country hurried to courts to demand new trials for clients on Death Rows. Executions were halted to allow the legal process to work.

The decisions did not shackle police and prosecutors, as many maintained. They simply took the premium off muscle and coercion and duplicity and placed it on intelligence and modern crime-fighting techniques.

The 1972 U. S. Supreme Court decision, which made the moratorium on the death sentence official, came when 631 persons were on Death Rows in 31 states and the District of Columbia. The lives of these persons were spared. So were the lives of 117 others whose cases were on appeal.

There were 45 men on Huntsville's Death Row at the time of the decision, and seven others were in county jails awaiting shipment to Huntsville. Though their sentences were commuted to life imprisonment, in most cases, some of the men continued to fight, arguing that they were not guilty in the first place, or that even life imprisonment was too harsh a penalty for their crimes.

One of those who continued to fight was Joe Edward Smith, now No. 228046 in the regular prison population, once No. 433 on Death Row. Smith wanted a new trial because he insisted he was innocent. He knew it was risky business because a verdict might be delivered at a time when a new capital punishment law could be ruled valid in Texas.

Smith, a small but husky black, spent a decade on Death Row—in the cell nearest to the execution chamber. He watched sixteen condemned men walk through the little green door. He was granted 21 reprieves. Some of them came at times when he already had "psyched himself up" to die. Once the executioner had already placed his hands on his equipment when the phone call came. Another time his life was spared because the Houston International Airport was fog-bound. The only transcript of Smith's case was to have been returned to Houston from Washington, D. C., the day before his scheduled execution for a federal judge to study. When the fog closed the airport and planes could not land, the judge issued a thirty-day stay of execution. The 21 reprieves left Smith with a tic at the corner of his mouth.

He was given the death sentence as a principal in one of the country's most sensationalized murder cases. Smith and six other young blacks were charged in 1959 with sexually molesting a twelve-year-old white boy and stuffing him in an old ice box in an abandoned shack on an otherwise vacant lot in Houston. The lot was in an area that contained a small black community. Police seemed always in the neighborhood to quell one kind of disturbance or another or to make some kind of criminal investigation. White youngsters venturing into the area were often attacked by groups of black youngsters.

When the white boy's body was first found in the ice box —he had been missing all night—a police hunt focused on a known child molester who was said to have exposed himself to two young girls some hours before the boy disappeared, and to have attempted to lure several small children into his auto. When this lead failed to pan out, police rounded up dozens of young black boys from the neighborhood. They finally settled on seven: Joe Edward Smith, who was seventeen; Adrian Johnson, seventeen; Charles Archer, fifteen; David Clemons, fifteen; Ira Lee Sadler, thirteen; and two brothers, Roy Eugene Miller, sixteen, and Robert Lee Miller, twelve.

Police said all of the boys confessed. The black community hired attorneys for the youths, and the seven immediately recanted. Adrian Johnson went to trial first. He said he was nowhere near the shack at the time of the assault-murder, but was eating cinnamon rolls at a cousin's house. His attorneys asked for a mistrial when a police captain admitted that he had removed the fingerprint chemicals from the ice box that very morning, and that Johnson's expert fingerprint witnesses would find no prints on the box. Police had said Johnson's prints were on the box. The motion for the mistrial was denied. Johnson was given the death penalty.

Joe Edward Smith went to trial. He vigorously denied being near the shack. He was arrested at home while watching television. Police had no warrant for his arrest. At police headquarters, Smith said, "they took me to a window and said I just might end up a suicide . . . so I confessed."

Smith was given the death penalty. His lawyer, Jo Ed Winfree, appealed on grounds that Smith's arrest was illegal and his confession forced. The conviction was affirmed. Winfree asked the U.S. Supreme Court for a writ of certiorari, but it was denied. Winfree sought a writ of habeas corpus from Federal Judge James Noel of the Southern District of Texas on grounds of an involuntary confession. Judge Noel turned it down. The denial was appealed to the U. S. Fifth Circuit Court of Appeals in New Orleans. It was rejected. Winfree went back to the U. S. Supreme Court for a writ of certiorari, and again was rejected. Winfree was aging and ill. He told Smith he had done all he could do. He died shortly thereafter.

By this time it was 1963; Smith had been incarcerated three years. At this point a young lawyer entered the case at the request of a white Houston couple who for years had fought for equal rights—Gould and Mary Beech. They feared that Smith was mentally retarded. The lawyer, James Hippard, obtained the services of a noted clinical psychologist who went to Death Row and gave Smith a battery of tests. The doctor's verdict: "Joe Edward Smith may be ignorant, but he certainly isn't dumb." So Hippard began "sizing up" the various decisions handed down by the U. S. Supreme Court in order to keep Smith alive while he could study the case and devise a defense.

"Here we had various young men picked up and all accused of this truly heinous crime," Hippard told me later, "yet no two of the defendants listed all the names of the defendants in their statements. One of the kids had a speech defect. The police had to interview him through his mother, who would converse with her son and relay the answers. Nobody could make heads or tails out of what he was saying except his mother. But when his confession was offered, it read in the finest of the king's English.

"And the facts didn't back up the confessions. The police reports indicated there had been no disturbance at all in the little abandoned shack. But with six or seven young boys scuffling around in such a little room, you'd think the dust, at least, would have been disturbed. After all, it was the headquarters for a dirt yard only two weeks before it was abandoned. And the fingerprints on the ice box—they had to belong to someone else, or they would not have been destroyed by the police.

"Now, in Joe Edward's case the state really had only

what I eventually claimed was an illegal confession, and some tenuous circumstantial evidence by Dr. Joseph Jachimczyk, the Harris County pathologist, that the white boy was 'bear hugged' to death.

"Adrian Johnson was convicted on the basis of a confession in which he described the white boy as "fighting and screaming" as he was stuffed into the ice box. Since Smith had not confessed to the crime, in fact had denied being on the scene, the state in Smith's case attempted to prove the opposite—that the white boy was dead before he was ever put into the box."

Hippard showed me a transcript of Dr. Jachimczyk's relevant testimony:

Q: Would the injuries that you found in the chest be compatible to a person's body being placed in a bear-hug or something about the body, that is, crushed in a bear-hug?

A: Yes, sir, the chest injury is compatible with that type of coerce.

Q: The cause of death was what?

A: Asphyxia, due to suffocation in association with sodomy.

Q: And that asphyxia would have been such that it could have been caused either by the choking and strangling him with hands, or something, and suffocating him by placing arms, hands, fingers over his nose and mouth, or by smothering him by squeezing and pressing his chest with arms and hands, is that correct?

A: Yes, sir.

Hippard filed an appeal to Federal Judge James Noel for a writ of habeas corpus. His brief asked, "What could be more unfair denial of due process than to send petitioner to his death without the state having introduced any evidence *legally* establishing that petitioner . . . committed the death-dealing acts alleged by the state, or even that the deceased, in fact, met his death in a manner contended by the state?

"It is incumbent upon the state . . . to introduce the

149

minimum proof required by Texas law for establishing a prima facie case. Especially was this true in the face of the appellant's vigorous and continued assertion that his written extra-judicial admission was forced from him, and in the face of his strong denial of any implication in the alleged crime. The state wholly failed to meet the minimum requirements of Texas law."

Judge Noel not only rejected Hippard's appeal for a writ of habeas corpus, but he refused another stay of execution for Smith. So Hippard appealed Judge Noel's decision to the U.S. Fifth Circuit Court of Appeals, citing the same arguments presented Judge Noel. He got another stay of execution for Smith (this was in 1964) to allow the jurists time to consider a decision (which, eventually, was against Smith).

But also in 1964 came a decision by the U.S. Supreme Court that saved Smith's life, and may, eventually, gain him freedom. The case, under the listing of "Jackson v. Denno," involved the admission as evidence of pre-trial confessions. The thrust of Jackson v. Denno was that a state could not introduce a confession into a trial without first establishing— out of the presence of the trial jury—that the confession had been made voluntarily. And that the issue of voluntariness must be determined specifically and concretely by the trial judge (or even by a separate jury), and that this determination must be a matter of the trial record. If the judge decided that the confession was a voluntary one, and allowed its introduction into a trial, the jury could in itself rule differently. If the judge decided the confession was an involuntary one, then the jury would never hear about it.

There had been no such hearing in the original trial before Judge Ed Duggan, and Hippard immediately began preparing another appeal to Federal Judge Noel asking for a Jackson v. Denno hearing on Smith's alleged confession. Judge Noel held a hearing of his own at which Judge Duggan testified that he had held the equivalent of a Jackson v. Denno hearing "in my own mind," and that he had decided Smith's confession was a voluntary one. Judge Noel thereupon rejected Hippard's request for an official Jackson v.

Denno hearing under the definition of the U. S. Supreme Court.

"The way Judge Duggan had done it—deciding in his mind that a confession was voluntary or forced—was the way it had been done in Texas in the past," Hippard said later. "In reality, the judge left it up to the jury to determine the legality of the confession. What I was asking was for Judge Noel to send the case back to the trial court on the basis that there had been no Jackson v. Denno hearing in Smith's trial as defined by the Supreme Court."

Rejected by Judge Noel, Hippard again turned to the Fifth Circuit Court of Appeals for relief, and in late 1964 he flew to Atlanta at his own expense to argue that Smith was entitled to a Jackson v. Denno hearing. Such a hearing, he felt sure, would bring Smith a new trial. Hippard had to wait for two and a half years before the Fifth Circuit handed down its determination—and it was a big one. The case was remanded back to Judge Duggan's original trial court and a Jackson v. Denno hearing by Judge Duggan was ordered.

Late in 1968 and in early 1969 a Jackson v. Denno hearing was held in Judge Duggan's court. Hippard also insisted on the judge hearing all the new decisions that had been handed down in the interim.

He claimed that Smith's confession had been obtained without benefit of an attorney's advice (Escabedo v. Illinois), that Smith had not been informed of his rights (Miranda v. Arizona), and that he had been tried by an illegally selected jury (Witherspoon v. Illinois).

And he stressed another argument, based on a decision in a case entitled Phelper v. Decker. He claimed that Smith had been illegally arrested, that as a direct result of this illegal arrest a confession had been obtained—and that the illegal arrest voided the confession.

Hippard also pointed out that Smith was just seventeen at the time of his arrest, was ignorant, could read at no better than a third grade level, had been held incommunicado for a number of days and not permitted to have visitors, and had not been allowed to read his own confession.

Judge Duggan still hewed to the line that he already had

held a Jackson v. Denno in his mind. And he still held that Smith's confession was voluntary.

So again, late in 1969, Hippard went back to Federal Judge Noel, seeking a writ of habeas corpus in a brief based on a series of questions. He felt a "yes" answer to the questions would almost automatically result in an overthrow of Judge Duggan's decision when measured by the yardstick of the recent decisions. Hippard asked:

1. Was Smith denied due process when Judge Duggan predetermined the voluntariness of the confession?
2. Does an illegal arrest render a confession constitutionally inadmissable?
3. Was, from the total circumstances, Smith's confession forced rather than freely made?
4. Did the hearing before Judge Duggan clearly establish that, in selecting the petitioner's jury, the state trial judge failed to make the searching inquiry required by Witherspoon?
5. Did the 1969 hearing before Duggan establish that a jury consisting only of jurors without scruples against the death penalty (such as the jury in the petitioner's case) is more prosecution prone, thus rendering petitioner's jury trial a denial of due process and equal protection of the law?
6. Were Smith's rights violated by the above?
7. Did Texas' practice of letting the jury impose the death penalty violate Smith's due process rights?
8. Did the Texas single-verdict procedure, which requires that a jury determine guilt and punishment simultaneously, and required Smith to choose between presenting mitigating evidence on the punishment issue or exercising his privilege against self-incrimination on the guilt issue, violate petitioner's constitutional rights under the 5th Amendment and 14th Amendment?

The brief concluded that the Fifth Circuit Court of Appeals had pointed out that the Miranda rule, although applying only indirectly in a case such as Smith's, does stress judicial skepticism in reviewing the contention that a man in custody, without legal counsel and faced only by his arresting officers, voluntarily waives his rights. Hippard asked application of this skepticism to Smith's case. He also concluded that results of the hearings before Judge Duggan on his request for a Jackson v. Denno hearing "clearly establish" Smith's rights to a new trial.

Federal Judge Noel received this request for a writ of habeas corpus in 1971. At this writing he has not ruled on it. Meanwhile, the U. S. Supreme Court released Smith from the shadow of the electric chair by its June 29, 1972 decision. Smith's death sentence was commuted to life in prison.

But Joe Edward Smith was not satisfied. "I did *not* participate in it," he reiterates to this day. "I want my freedom!"

Smith told me that his dictionary, a popsicle stick and a "little white lie" kept him from going insane during his long years on Death Row. He was further buoyed by constant visits by his mother and sister, and the persistent efforts of Hippard, now an associate professor of law at the University of Houston.

"When I got here I had gone through the fourth grade in school," Smith told me a few years ago, "but I really couldn't read and write. One day my mother brought me a book. It was *Don Quixote.* When I tried to read it, it was like trying to make sense out of hen tracks. So I got hold of a dictionary from a chaplain. I started through the book, checking out the words I couldn't understand with the dictionary. I've run through quite a few dictionaries, incidentally. And Howard Stickney left me one of his Bibles."

As Smith thumbed through his dictionary, year in and year out, the task of educating himself became progressively easier. Attorney Hippard's thesaurus helped immeasurably. But Smith's mental outlook began to deteriorate.

"It was the depression that used to get me," he said. "One time I was so far gone that I even tried to kick down the door, but I only hurt my leg. I was pleased, anyway, because I found I wasn't becoming just a vegetable; I could react to something, even if it was just a hurt leg.

"One day I decided to do something about this getting the blues. I took a popsicle stick and taped it to the steel bar over the door. I made it my good luck piece, my inspiration, and whenever I would get blue, or real depressed, or mad at the world, I'd look up at that popsicle stick and it would tell me to 'settle down, Joe Edward,' and I would.

"That time I got so close to going down? That was the time I told a little white lie. My mother, my uncle and a sister were visiting me. It was my execution day, my last day. I forget which execution day it was. But my folks were sitting there in front of my cell door when they began to test the generators.

"It was about ten or eleven o'clock in the morning. My sister noticed the whine of the generators and she looked at me and said, 'Joe Edward, what's that sound?'

"I could see the panic creeping in her eyes, and hear it in her voice. I just told her that one of the suction fans bringing in fresh air was acting up. I don't think my mother and uncle noticed the noise too much because they were too busy talking to me about another reprieve they thought sure would come through.

"I spent most of that visit trying to cheer up my mother, reassuring her the stay would come through. But then, after everyone was gone, and I had been shaved and had taken a shower, and that reprieve didn't come along—well, things got pretty grim.

"And by eleven o'clock that night I figured it was the end and I got to psychin' myself up to take the walk. Death Row is not the noisiest place on an execution day, and it was absolutely dead silent that night. And then, with just a few minutes to go, the telephone rang. I about died from the shock!" Smith grinned wryly; even recalling the harrowing experience had left him in a sweat. The tic twitched.

Several years after the psychologist told Hippard that "Joe Edward may be ignorant, but he certainly isn't dumb," Hippard took Smith books for a Christmas present. "When I handed them to him through the bars he looked sort of sheepish, and I understood that he had read the books," Hippard told me.

Smith has read many books since the day his mother gave him the copy of *Don Quixote,* and he can quote the book page after page. And the Bible also. He took correspondence courses in a variety of subjects for a number of years, and after his sentence was commuted he enrolled in classes in the Windham Independent School District, a unique school program inside the prison system. In 1973 he completed the equivalent of the tenth grade. He intends to receive the equivalent of a high school diploma . . . in or out of prison.

Of the seven defendants, Adrian Johnson was executed and Smith is doing time on a life sentence. What of the other five?

Charles Archer, fifteen, was tried—and a psychiatrist testified that Archer didn't know the difference between right and wrong ninety percent of the time. He was sent to a reformatory. That was in 1959. In 1970 he was declared sane, and was freed under a federal court ruling that a person cannot be tried as an adult on a charge for which he had been tried as a juvenile.

David Clemons, fifteen, was convicted in 1959 and sentenced to a reformatory. He was released in 1963.

Ira Sadler, thirteen, was declared a delinquent. He had been sent to a reformatory at the age of nine. He was returned there as a parole violator. He was released in 1968 under the federal court ruling which applied in the Charles Archer case.

Roy and Robert Miller, the brothers, sixteen and twelve at the time of the murder, were declared delinquent and sent to a reformatory. Roy was released in 1962, Robert in 1967.

The U. S. Supreme Court decision of June 29, 1972 on capital punishment said, generally, that the death sentence as it had been administered until that date was unlawful because it had been handed down improperly. It was a five-to-four decision. Three of the justices in the majority seemed to hold capital punishment unconstitutional because of its nature as a cruel and unusual form of punishment. The other two in the majority found it to be cruel and unusual but only because it had been "capriciously" imposed in a "trivial" number of cases. "Indeed, it smacks of little more than a lottery system," said Justice William J. Brennan, Jr.

The dissenting justices felt generally that to retain or abolish capital punishment was a decision the people should make through their state legislatures. This feeling prevailed, for the ruling left the way open for states to continue to impose the death penalty if legislatures can write new laws which would apply capital punishment with uniformity and without "caprice."

These nine men had been bombarded with every argument for and against capital punishment. How they sifted through the arguments to arrive at such a dangling decision is apparent in some of the words and sentences in the individual opinions they offered when the vote was taken. The remarks are interesting even if, to me, the failure to decisively outlaw the death penalty was depressing.

Those voting to halt imposition of the death penalty were Potter Stewart, William J. Brennan, Jr., Byron R. White, William O. Douglas and Thurgood Marshall.

Stewart said in part: "The penalty of death differs from all other forms of criminal punishment, not in degree but in kind. It is unique in its total irrevocability. It is unique in its rejection of rehabilitation of the convict as a basic purpose of criminal justice. And it is unique, finally, in its absolute renunciation of all that is embodied in our concept of humanity . . . .

"These death sentences are cruel and unusual in the same way that being struck by lightning is cruel and unusual. For, of all the people convicted of rapes and murders in 1967 and 1968, many just as reprehensible as these, the petitioners are among a capriciously selected random handful upon whom the sentence of death has in fact been imposed . . . ."

Brennan said in part: "It is a denial of human dignity for the state arbitrarily to subject a person to an unusually severe punishment that society has indicated it does not regard as acceptable and that cannot be shown to serve any penal purpose more effectively than a significantly less drastic punishment. Under these principles and this test, death is today a 'cruel and unusual' punishment . . . .

"When the punishment of death is inflicted in a trivial number of cases in which it is legally available, the conclusion is virtually inescapable that it is being inflicted arbitrarily. Indeed, it smacks of little more than a lottery system . . . .

"The punishment of death cannot be justified as a necessary means of exacting retribution from criminals. When the overwhelming number of criminals who commit capital crimes go to prison, it cannot be concluded that death serves the purpose of retribution more effectively than imprisonment. The asserted public belief that murderers and rapists deserve to die is flatly inconsistent with the execution of a random few . . . our society wishes to prevent crime; we have no desire to kill criminals simply to get even with them . . . ."

White said in part: "The death penalty is exacted with great infrequency even for the most atrocious crimes and . . . there is no meaningful basis for distinguishing the few cases in which it is imposed from the many cases in which it is not. The short of it is that the policy of vesting sentencing authority primarily in juries—a decision largely motivated by the desire to mitigate the harshness of the law and to bring community judgment to bear on the sentence as well as guilt or innocence—has so effectively achieved its aims that capital punishment within the confines of the statutes now before us has for all practical purposes run its course . . . ."

Douglas said in part: "In a nation committed to equal protection of the laws, there is no permissible 'caste' aspect of law enforcement. Yet we know that the discretion of judges and juries in imposing the death penalty enables the penalty to be selectively applied, feeding prejudices against the accused if he is poor and despised, poor and lacking in political clout, or if he is a member of a suspect or unpopular minority, and saving those who by social position may be in a more protected position . . . .

"A law that stated that anyone making more than

$50,000 would be exempt from the death penalty would plainly fall, as would a law that in terms said that blacks, those who never went beyond the fifth grade in school, or those who made less than $3,000 a year, or those who were unpopular or unstable would be the only people executed. A law which in the overall view reaches that result in practice has no more sanctity than a law which in terms provides the same . . . ."

Marshall said in part: "In striking down capital punishment, this court does not malign our system of government. On the contrary, it pays homage to it. Only in a free society could right triumph in difficult times, and could civilization record its magnificent advancement. In recognizing the humanity of our fellow beings, we pay ourselves the highest tribute. We achieve a major milestone in the long road up from barbarism and join the approximately seventy other jurisdictions in the world which celebrate their regard for civilization and humanity by shunning capital punishment . . . ."

Those justices dissenting were Chief Justice Warren E. Burger, William H. Rehnquist, Harry A. Blackmun and Lewis F. Powell, Jr.

Blackmun said in part: "I yield to no one in the depth of my distaste, antipathy, and, indeed, abhorrence, for the death penalty . . . that distaste is buttressed by a belief that capital punishment serves no useful purpose that can be demonstrated. For me, it violates childhood's training and life's experiences, and is not compatible with the philosophical convictions I have been able to develop. It is antagonistic to any sense of 'reverence for life.' Were I a legislator, I would vote against the death penalty . . . .

"Our task here . . . is to pass upon the constitutionality of legislation that has been enacted and that is challenged. This is the sole task of judges. We should not allow our personal preferences as to the wisdom of legislation and congressional action, or our distaste for such action, to guide our judicial decision in cases such as these.

"Although personally I may rejoice at the court's result, I find it difficult to accept or to justify as a matter of history, of law, or of constitutional pronouncement. I fear the court has overstepped. It has sought and has achieved an end . . . ."

Powell said in part: "In terms of the constitutional role of this court, the impact of the majority's ruling is all the greater because the decision encroaches upon an area squarely within the historic prerogative of the legislative branch—both state and federal—to protect the citizenry through the designation of penalties for prohibitable conduct. It is the very sort of judgment that the legislative branch is competent to make and for which the judiciary is ill-equipped. Throughout our history, justices of this court have emphasized the gravity of decisions invalidating legislative judgments, admonishing the nine men who sit on this bench of the duty of self-restraint, especially when called upon to apply the expansive due process and cruel and unusual punishment rubrics. I can recall no case in which, in the name of deciding constitutional questions, this court has subordinated national and local democratic processes to such an extent . . . ."

Rehnquist said in part: "The court's judgment today strikes down a penalty our nation's legislators have thought necessary since our country was founded. My brothers Douglas, Brennan and Marshall would at one fell swoop invalidate laws enacted by Congress and forty of the fifty state legislatures and would consign to the limbo of unconstitutionality . . . penalties for offenses as varied and unique as murder, piracy, mutiny, hijacking and desertion in the face of the enemy . . . .

"The task of judging constitutional cases . . . cannot be avoided, but it must surely be approached with the deepest humility and genuine deference to legislative judgment. Today's decision . . . is significantly lacking in those attributes . . . this decision holding unconstitutional capital punishment is not an act of judgment, but rather an act of will . . . ."

Chief Justice Burger voiced what I considered the damning feature of the decision: "The future of capital punishment in this country has been left in an uncertain limbo. Rather than providing a final and unambiguous answer on the basic constitutional question, the collective impact of the majority's ruling is to demand an undetermined measure of change from the various state legislatures and the Congress . . . .

"The legislatures are free to eliminate capital punishment for specific crimes or to carve out limited exceptions to a general abolition of the penalty. While I would not undertake to make a more definitive statement as to the parameters of the court's ruling, it is clear that if state legislatures and the Congress wish to maintain the availability of capital punishment, significant statutory changes will have to be made. Legislative bodies may seek to bring their laws into compliance with the court's ruling by providing standards for juries and judges to follow in determining the sentence in capital cases or by more narrowly defining the crimes for which the penalty is to be imposed . . . ."

A third of the state legislatures at this writing were doing just that—passing laws they hoped would satisfy the Court's requirements. And President Richard Nixon asked Congress to authorize "automatic" death penalties for wartime treason, sabotage and espionage, and for federal crimes such as skyjacking and kidnaping in which death results. He said the Justice Department was convinced his proposals would be constitutional. He added, "The sharp reduction in the application of the death penalty was a component of the more permissive attitude toward crime in the last decade . . . ."

Obviously, Nixon did not have the benefit of studies made by various groups and arms of government when he spoke.

It seems likely that the Supreme Court will not overrule reasonable attempts by the states or Congress to reinstate the death sentence. Polls taken soon after the Supreme Court decision showed that 57 percent of those questioned favored the death penalty for persons convicted of murder. To meet the Supreme Court's requirements, all persons convicted of murder would need to be executed—and therein lies the rub. A mandatory death sentence for all convicted of murder would satisfy the Court's criteria, but juries would falter. It is one thing to tell a pollster you favor the death penalty; it is another to sit on a jury and hand it down. And it is foolish to suppose that the people Justice Douglas wrote of—"those who by social position may be in a more protected position"—would countenance watching persons from the higher socio-economic strata walk to the electric chair. In short, restricted capital punishment—capital punishment for a narrow field of crimes—would be the same old capital punishment, for only those from the lower socio-economic groups would die, no matter how few the crimes for which the death sentence was mandatory.

Legislatures are feeling pressure from law enforcement officers, most of whom feel much like Los Angeles Police Chief Edward Davis, who said after the 1972 decision: "The decision is an absurdity that violates any plain, simple country boy's interpretation of the Constitution . . . ."

Fortunately, the interpretation of the Constitution is not left to "plain, simple" country boys, some of whom may happen to be chiefs of police. Unfortunately, these "plain, simple" country boys have the lung power and political clout to impress legislators. And a vast majority of legislators know no more about the facts of capital punishment and its administration than a hog knows about a holiday. And it cares no more.

10

Losers and Winners

Put a derby on Carroll Farrar's head and he was ringer for Stan Laurel of Laurel and Hardy fame. He was a little guy, not much over five feet tall, and he weighed about 125 pounds. He had a perkiness about him that brought smiles to the prison population, inmates and official personnel alike. He worked in the prison dining room, and he worked hard. He also obeyed the rules. He was serving a five-year sentence for statutory rape. He was married and the father of two children.

I didn't deliberately "observe" Farrar, but it was impossible over the months not to notice how he stood out among the general run of prisoners. He had attracted the attention of O.B. Ellis, then the prison system general manager, and Ellis and I often talked of him. One day I suggested that Ellis have Farrar's background thoroughly investigated. "I think the guy deserves a chance in the free world, if his background is clean," I said.

Ellis, one of the genuinely effective men in prison administration, saw that the investigation was conducted. "He'll do," Ellis told me, "and I think I can get him a job in Houston." He got the job for Farrar—working in a carwash for $40 a week. Ellis pushed for parole, parole was granted and Farrar left prison to earn his complete freedom.

Months passed by. In the rush of daily events I forgot Carroll Farrar. Then, one morning over breakfast coffee, I was stunned by a story on the front page of the *Houston Post*. Farrar had killed a policeman after robbing a liquor store! I couldn't believe it. I couldn't picture the little man with a pistol in his hand. I reached for the phone to call Ellis, but pulled my hand back. Ellis would be as dismayed as I was. Our efforts had ended in wretched failure.

I was a younger man when this occurred, and I felt more than dismay. I felt resentment. Farrar had let me down, had let Ellis down. The feeling persisted while Farrar was quickly tried, quickly convicted and quickly shipped to Death Row. Ellis and I pored over the reports of the investigation of Farrar's background Ellis had ordered. Nowhere was there any evidence that Farrar had ever used firearms or threatened to use them. No charges had ever been filed against him except the one for statutory rape.

Still, I didn't want to talk with Farrar. The resentment was still there, the feeling that Farrar had made me play the fool, the feeling that I had played the fool out of a sense of self-importance.

But one day I had to go. Whatever emotion impelled me toward his cell door, I was almost angry by the time I reached it. I had it in my mind to rap on the bars and demand, "What the hell is wrong with you, Farrar?" But Farrar saw me as I entered Death Row. He bounded to the cell door. "Now, wait a minute, Mr. Reid! Don't go judging me. Let me tell you what happened first."

I pulled up a chair and told him to start talking.

Farrar spoke rapidly. The carwash manager had cheated him. He had promised Ellis he would pay Farrar $40 a week. Farrar's wife had taken a job as a waitress. She had set up a budget based on the promised $40 and her salary and tips. The budget was small but enough, she calculated, to take care of them and the two children.

"At the end of my first week he gave me twenty dollars," Farrar said. "I asked him why. He told me, 'Now, what do you expect? You're an ex-con. If you don't like it, if you don't like the job, I'll turn you in. Take it or leave it.'"

I said, "Why in the hell didn't you call me or Mr. Ellis? We could have stopped that right there. We could have got you another job." Farrar began shaking his head—and I realized how silly I had sounded. His parole supervisor was the Salvation Army under the rules of the system. But his real supervisor was his employer.

"I couldn't even look for another job," Farrar said. "I couldn't afford to make him mad. So I rocked along, getting the twenty a week, and we kept getting deeper in debt, and I guess I kept getting a little sorer about it all."

In prison Farrar had heard that liquor stores were easy to rob. There was one next door to the grocery store where he traded. He bought a cheap pistol in a pawn shop. He set out for the liquor store with the pistol in his waistband and hidden by his coat.

"I don't know why, but I dropped into the grocery store," Farrar said. "I guess I wasn't such a hot holdup man, because the manager noticed the bulge under my coat. He'd been around long enough to figure what was making the bulge. He knew I was on parole, and he knew I was up to something. I left the grocery store and walked next door to the liquor store. It was no trouble at all getting the money. The holdup went off all right. But when I headed out the door, here was this policeman coming right toward me."

Farrar paused, remembering. "I absolutely froze for a second. I was so scared I almost pissed my pants. All I could think of was, 'I'm not going back to that penitentiary!' I jumped toward a little alleyway beside the liquor store and ran through it and wound up in a parking lot. I could hear sirens and I knew more cops were on the way."

Farrar shook his head and sighed. "The good Lord knows I didn't want to shoot that policeman. I wanted a chance to duck through the cars and get away, so I fired at him to scare him so I could get the chance. But damn it, the other cops had got there, and he raised up and ran right into the bullet. I threw down my gun and raised my hands." He grimaced like Stan Laurel and rubbed knuckles across his eyes.

The jury had heard testimony about the robbery and the shootout. A policeman had been killed. That had been enough to bring a quick conviction and the death sentence. I determined that the other parts of the story—the events before the robbery—were going to be heard. Not that the telling could help Farrar. It could help others.

Farrar put that funny, hopeful little Stan Laurel smile on his face as he went through the little green door. His battle jacket was too large for him, and it pouched up around his ears like an inflated life preserver when he sat down in the chair.

Farrar was what prison administrators call a "recidivist" —an ex-convict who commits other crimes after his release and is returned to prison. A repeater.

Society says its penal systems are in business to punish wrongdoers, to isolate the wrongdoers until the punishment brings about a change in attitude, and then to rehabilitate the wrongdoers so that they will sin no more when they are returned to the free world. This is what society says.

Before Carroll Farrar was executed in 1956, Texas had no parole system worthy of the name. It had no viable rehabilitation program. It had the beginning of a pre-release program. After I had written my story for the AP about Farrar's execution, I sat down and wrote the story of what had occurred before the robbery and sent it to the Parole Board with a copy to the Department of Corrections. And I sent along a list of recommendations for instituting a genuine parole system.

The volunteer system the state was using simply wasn't working, I pointed out. Many of the volunteers were kind-hearted persons, acquaintances or even relatives of the parolees, but they knew nothing in the way of keeping tabs on their wards, and seldom had the time or understanding to worry with a parolee's singular problems. Some volunteers were employers seeking cheap labor. Others were criminals who wanted to obtain release of experienced men for future criminal enterprises.

The recidivist had become a major prison problem, I wrote, and certainly a major problem for the state. They made up more than a third of the prison population, and imposed a strain on the ability of the prison system to absorb a steadily increasing flow of new inmates. They cost the citizens millions in losses from robbery, theft and burglary.

There were many things to be done to solve this problem, I wrote, but the first thing was to install an intelligent parole system.

Steps were taken to install such a system, but they were hesitant steps. Legislators who couldn't see beyond the ends of their noses snorted about the cost. Others didn't want to be accused of "coddling criminals."

Crawford Martin and several other powerful legislators were to be guests at the Texas Press Association's annual meeting, and I decided to plead my case with them if possible. At the meeting I drew aside Martin and State Senator A.M. Aikin, Jr. I plunged into my argument with a full head of steam.

When I was through, Martin frowned at me. "Just what are you getting out of this, Reid?"

Neither Martin nor Aikin ever knew how much restraint I exercised, for my fists clenched to smash his nose. I exploded verbally instead. "Listen, you two! I paid my own way to this affair. I haven't been standing around drinking free whiskey. I've paid for mine. If there's a payoff connected with everything in Austin, you know more about that sort of thing than I do. I'm talking to you about something that needs to be done—before things get worse! Can't you understand that?"

Martin was not taken aback by my outburst. He waited a moment for my anger to cool, then said, "I didn't know you felt this strongly about it, Don. I was a fool awhile ago. I know how much experience you've had, and I know how much information you have. I tell you now we'll take a hard look at your recommendations and see what we can do."

Martin and Aikin did plenty. With their strong support, the parole revision plan was voted in. Professional parole supervisors were employed. Supervisors now investigate prospective employers, check on wages promised—and paid. They keep tabs on parolees—their conduct, their habits and acquaintances. They make reports to the Parole Board. And they do something else. Their knowledge of the problems facing the ex-con gives them a better opportunity to lend a helping hand or a listening ear.

If Carroll Farrar had been able to explain to a responsible parole supervisor that his employer had refused to pay him his promised wage, Farrar may not have robbed the liquor store and killed the police officer. In my opinion, Farrar with proper supervision would have made as good a citizen as the most of us are. We all know how good that is, don't we?

In 1961 a man named George Beto took charge of the prison system. For six years prior to that time he had been secretary of the Department of Corrections. He was brilliant, hard-headed and compassionate. No con ever conned him, and none ever failed to get his help if help was deserved. He also was articulate and persuasive; when he spoke, legislators listened.

Beto made the pre-release program work. His aim was to prepare an inmate for life in the outside world. He knew that many prisoners had been behind walls for years, that they had no idea of the changes which had occurred outside. A pre-release center was set up at the Beauford Jester unit near Sugarland. Since the primary concern of a man or woman seeking release is the ability to get a job and keep it, Beto invited businessmen of all kinds to the center to talk with inmates. State employment agencies also sent representatives. Businessmen were surprised at the amount of talent they found among the inmates. Inmates were surprised to find businessmen interested in their talents.

But Beto did more than this. He had insurance men come to the center to explain how different programs worked. He coaxed income tax experts to the center to lecture. Inmates were told how to buy an automobile, how to rent an apartment or rent or buy a house. They were told how to keep healthy in a new environment, and how to maintain emotional balance. Beto even had fashion experts come in with color movies to show the men and women how people dressed in the free world. And he called on me to lecture on what he called "human relations." The program lasts four to six weeks, and inmates are given a 136-page manual to study as a supplement to the "live" courses.

The program at first was limited to inmates on the verge of discharge. It was so successful that Beto broadened the classes to include selected parole prospects. As a result, all dischargees and parolees now pass through the center prior to release.

The parole system and the pre-release program worked better than even their strongest advocates had expected, but it was the Windham Independent School District that fast became the pride and joy of Beto and the entire Department of Corrections. It is a full-fledged school district operated entirely inside prison walls. It is some 200 miles long and as wide as the "open concept" teaching facilities used in plugging the academic and vocational gaps in the lives of 7,500 inmate students. It has no taxing authority; it is funded through the Texas Board of Education, which allocates state funds to all of the state's school districts.

Members of the Texas Board of Corrections serve as the district's school board. The district hires its own teachers and staff, and the same qualifications and certification is required as is required by other school districts. The Windham system is manned by more than 170 teachers and staff. They teach in classrooms or "open concept" quarters provided in each of the prison system units. Each unit is assigned its own staff, with system headquarters in the Huntsville central unit. The teaching staff—men and women—is integrated (the Eastham unit has a black principal). There are bilingual instructors in all three areas of instruction—academic, vocational and special education. Due to the large number of Mexican-American inmates, Windham is always seeking more qualified bilingual teachers and staff members.

The curriculum for Windham is laid out along two parallel lines—academic and vocational. On the academic side, it stresses development of basic reading and mathematical skills of illiterate inmates, and broadens the knowledge of the severely under-educated. It also prepares qualified inmates to pass the General Educational Development (GED) tests for the equivalent of high school diplomas, and strengthens the academic skills of inmates preparing to enter college.

Long-time inmates may follow through to obtain junior college degrees in a companion program that utilizes instructional facilities of four nearby junior colleges.

From a vocational standpoint, the district offers more than a score of courses designed to provide the unskilled inmate with a trade that will enable him to earn a living. These include appliance repair, auto-body work, cabinet making, drafting, cosmetology, electrical equipment trades, horticulture, masonry, meat cutting (the prison system raises its own beef), painting and redecorating, radiator repair, radio and television repair, sheet metal work, air conditioning, and welding.

The entire Windham Independent School District concept was developed under Beto's direction. He was unhappy, to say the least, with the educational program he found when he assumed command of the prison system.

The average educational achievement level of the entire prison population was that of the fifth grade.

The average "IQ" was just eighty (but this rose to ninety when the system began receiving better educated young "dope users").

Eighteen percent of the prison population was mentally retarded.

Fifteen percent were functional illiterates unable to cope with problems that required more than a fifth-grade education for their solving.

Eighty-five percent were school dropouts.

Beto matched these depressing findings with another set of statistics that make all prison administrators wince—the rate of recidivism. Forty percent of the system population was made up of repeaters.

To Beto this was both a shocking waste of human lives and a costly burden to society. Texas was then spending approximately $1,200 a year to house, clothe and feed just one convict. The "repeaters" in the system totaled approximately 4,000 at the time; they cost the taxpayers some $5,000,000 annually.

Texas had an educational system that functioned in the overall rehabilitation process, but it fell considerably short of the standards Beto felt were necessary for a meaningful, worthwhile rehabilitation program. So he set out to devise a program, based upon this analysis of the prison population and its needs, that would, if successful, provide a truly productive rehabilitation program.

The answer lay in creation of a non-geographical school district within the Texas Department of Corrections. Beto went to the legislature with a simple bill creating such a district. It was approved and funds were provided to get the program in motion. It was called Windham Independent School District in honor of the Board of Correction's vice-chairman, James M. Windham of Livingston, Texas.

Legally, the legislation creating the district made every inmate of the Texas prison system a "scholastic." This is the basis on which state educational funds are distributed. But most of the inmates were over 21, the age limit where state responsibility stops. This raised the problem of funding the district. The state attorney general, however, approved the legislation and agreed that, in this instance, it was the responsibility of the state to offer educational facilities to inmates over 21. This opened the door to financing the education of prison inmates.

"We had one big factor going for us, Don," Beto said to me recently as we sat and talked about the past. "It was the atmosphere of discipline, of work and of education we had developed over the years. It was almost as if we had anticipated what we would try to do. Of the three, I feel prison discipline was the most important." I had to agree.

I remember when the district hired its first employee, the superintendent. Dr. Lane Murray was an attractive, brown-eyed woman, and eyebrows were lifted around the state when she assumed command. It was she who installed the "open school" concept and expanded the program unit by unit until thirteen of the fifteen units had fully developed facilities. It was an article of faith with her that an inmate who could learn to read well and add could assume responsibility for his progress.

Students in the academic program attend classes one day a week—and this is mandatory for any inmate, male or female, with less than a fifth-grade education. Attendance is on a voluntary basis for those with more than a fifth-grade education. But since conditions in an air-conditioned classroom or "open concept" learning center are immeasurably superior to those involving prison labor assignments on a prison farm under the hot Texas sun, most young inmates attend classes voluntarily. However, an inmate with a high school diploma is not eligible to attend Windham school district; he may participate in programs for higher degrees.

Vocational classes are conducted under a different schedule. Students taking these courses attend daily classes for six months, for a total of 880 hours, as they learn trades and skills that will enable them to get and hold jobs once they leave prison.

In addition, many semi-illiterates are placed in special classes with a low teacher-student ratio, especially designed materials and methods, and individually developed prescriptions for learning needs. This program extends over into another area of special education—schooling the retarded and emotionally disturbed.

A student attends classes on a non-graded basis, which allows him to advance at his own rate of achievement. Standard achievement tests are given thrice annually. There are no failures; some students just advance faster than others.

"We are graduating more than a thousand students a year now," Dr. Murray told me recently. "We hold three graduation ceremonies annually. We feel we are achieving some degree of success because more than 7,500 out of the prison population of 16,000 are attending academic and vocational classes."

Dr. Murray proudly pointed out a new development: credits earned at Windham can be transferred so an inmate can receive his high school diploma from his hometown high school. This program stems from the recent numbers of high school students sent to prison on narcotics charges.

"Lots of kids are getting busted today before they graduate because of dope incidents," Dr. Murray told me. "They may need a year's credits for their diploma, or only a semester's or so. With the State Commissioner of Education's office we have developed our own diploma plan. And all school districts have been asked to cooperate. We get an inmate's transcript from his high school, then tailor our curriculum to fit his needs for his diploma. When he has earned his needed credits, we send them back to his high school and the student can—if he wants to—get his diploma from his old school. We think this is important in aiding in the inmate's rehabilitation because it lets him know we are thinking of him as a human being and not just as a number."

In a parallel action, beginning in 1973, an inmate can graduate from the Windham Independent School District, receive a Windham diploma and class ring carrying the specially designed Windham seal, and the Texas Department of Corrections is never mentioned. "In fact," Dr. Murray said, "the Department of Corrections is never even mentioned in the graduation programs."

Windham district glamorizes its graduation exercises. Outstanding citizens and public figures are invited to deliver the graduation addresses, and each graduate may invite three members of his or her family to ceremonies, and these family members are honored, too.

"Getting that high school diploma may be the first thing the inmate student did that was ever worthwhile," said Dr. Murray. "He is proud of this, his family is proud of him, as we are, and his graduation is a big event. We do our best to make it a standout, meaningful occasion."

I am particularly proud of a program in progress at the Ferguson unit of the prison system. First offenders are placed there, and they stay there until they are 21. They are isolated from the regular prison population. They are tested and their rehabilitation needs determined. Actually, these youngsters are rehabilitation-oriented from the very day they begin to serve time. If they work and study hard, they can be rehabilitated and released without ever having to serve a day in the regular prison population. And this occurs with wonderful regularity.

The school district also brought another benefit to the entire prison system. All prison libraries were placed under the school district's authority. This assured that all libraries would hold volumes necessary to the development of the rehabilitation program—and it allowed Beto and Dr. Murray to install and expand what they call their "humanities concept."

They both know that all reading opens the eyes of inmates to behavioral patterns often completely foreign to them. They feel this will lead to broader knowledge and understanding of life in general which, in turn, will guide the inmate toward more intelligent ways and means of solving problems than the gun, the knife and the club. Good libraries, of course, also help make life bearable for inmates, especially long-termers.

What did all this cost the taxpayer? The upgrading of the pre-release program cost practically nothing. The manpower, for the most part, was already available. Only the adoption of new procedures and techniques was needed. As for the Windham Independent School District, its 1974 budget barely exceeds $2,000,000—and this after four years of operation.

But this is what is important: prison officials knew that a ten percent reduction in recidivism would save taxpayers almost $1,250,000 annually, based on the cost of maintaining a convict in prison for one year. Before the programs were installed and the school district founded, the rate of recidivism was 41 percent. By early 1973 the rate of recidivism had dropped to thirty percent for the entire prison population of some 16,000. And the rate of recidivism for the some 7,500 inmates involved in the rehabilitation programs had dropped to an astonishing seventeen percent! A financial burden was being lifted off the taxpayers' backs, and the poor and ignorant were receiving belated educations and learning skills and trades that demonstrably would help them find and hold jobs in the free world!

The Texas prison system was showing the real way to deter crime, and officials from other states were visiting Huntsville all during 1973 to study and learn. It warmed my heart to observe the pilgrimage.

Beto left the prison system recently. But he remained in Huntsville, on the faculty of Sam Houston State University. After a talk with him not long ago, my thoughts ran back to two men I had got to know well on Death Row.

One was Nolan West, a shy, quiet little man of 25, unschooled and unskilled, a petty thief who made a major mistake. West always looked as if he were expecting someone to speak harshly to him. Looking at him, you would not suspect that he had found the temerity to handle a pistol. But one night he borrowed a pistol in Houston—and used it. He was fresh out of the Dallas jail and in Houston visiting a friend. In a neighborhood tavern he spied a man named Blondy Parker, owner of jukeboxes about town. Jukebox operators in those days often dealt in other coin devices, some illegal, and West figured Parker would "rob easy" if he were in that category. Parker obviously had money because he was spending freely.

West borrowed the pistol. He crouched on the back seat floorboard of Parker's car. He planned to rise up and rob Parker once the car was underway. But inside the tavern, Parker handed his keys to an employee, Walter Zabaroski, and sent him on an errand.

So it was that when West rose up to rob Parker, Zabaroski was at the wheel. And Zabaroski was not the kind to "rob easy." His right hand darted for the glove compartment and the pistol in it. West panicked. He pushed open the rear door and began clawing his way out of the car. But Zabaroski, in reaching for the glove compartment, inadvertently jerked on the steering wheel. The car turned sharply and West went flying out of the door. His pistol fired. The bullet struck Zabaroski in the head.

West fled into the night but was captured a few days later. He quickly confessed. His trial was brief. His court-appointed lawyer offered no defense. The jury gave him the death penalty.

West took the "Jesus Route" more effectively than any inmate I ever saw. He was absolutely mesmerized by the time his execution date rolled around. He walked through the little green door on a euphoric cloud. He peered shyly at the men gathered in the Death House, then looked away, embarrassed.

As he moved nearer the chair, West stumbled slightly. Quickly he bobbed his head and smiled a soft apology for his clumsiness and the discomfiture he had caused his captors by interrupting the ritual.

He had no words for anyone. The guards strapped him in the chair. He blinked as the electrodes were placed.

But as a guard's hands came up to stuff his nostrils with cotton, West's eyes widened as awful realization swept away the euphoria. It was as if he had said to himself, "Why, these sons of bitches are going to kill me!" His lips parted to shriek out the panic in his soul.

And then a strange and marvelous thing occurred. Standing near West and just to the side of me was Father Duffy, that great, good man. He leaned forward a bit at the waist. He shook his head slightly—and winked at Nolan West. "No, Nolan," his wink and headshake said. "Everything is going to be all right."

West stared at him. Then his mouth closed, his features smoothed out, and to his lips came a faint and knowing smile. It was there when the executioner did his job.

The other man I thought of on that particular day was J. W. (Brazos) Morrow, a one-eyed giant of a man with a poet's love of the language, a romantic whose adoration of a Houston woman cost his life and the life of another man. Like Nolan West, Morrow had been in one kind of trouble or another since boyhood. He was paroled from Texas after serving three years for burglary. He violated his parole and went to Michigan where he served another three years for burglary, then was returned to Texas as a parole violator.

Because he had a commanding presence, an air of authority and a way with words, Morrow was almost immediately made a "trusty" and given a job as motion-picture projector operator. He traveled from unit to unit showing movies, spending as much as a month or more at each place. It was at Blue Ridge unit south of Houston that he first saw the red-haired woman who stole his heart. She was visiting a relative. Morrow, because he had a comparative freedom to move about, wooed her on her every visit to Blue Ridge. She was not an uneducated woman. She shared his love for classical music, poetry, and they talked of the wines they would share once Morrow gained freedom. She did not tell Morrow how she earned her living.

Morrow was so smitten, so eager to make love to the woman, that every moment in prison became torture to him. One night he broke into the prison armory, stole three pistols and a rifle, slipped past the guards and set off along the Southern Pacific tracks for Houston, some fifteen miles away. The woman was there.

About midnight he came upon a small Southern Pacific installation on the outskirts of Houston. Sitting by the yellow frame structure was a brand new Chevrolet. Inside the shack were Deputy Sheriff Eddie Shofner and his wife. Shofner had bought the car that day as a birthday present for his wife, who worked in the railroad shack. He had surprised her with the fine gift, and now they were talking about the future.

Morrow, bristling with firepower, burst through the door. He didn't want money, just the keys to the new car. Shofner, with more courage than caution, went for his revolver. Morrow fired his rifle. Shofner slumped to the floor. Morrow turned and fled—without the keys. Mrs. Shofner called police, then cradled her dying husband's head in her arms as she knelt beside him. She was like that when police arrived.

A dragnet of police, deputies and prison guards surrounded Morrow in the early morning near a huge electrical power complex and slowly moved in. Bloodhounds caught his scent and pointed to where he crouched in the shadows of the gaunt steel structures. Morrow weighed the odds, placed his weapons on the ground and waved his surrender.

At his trial the district attorney, to show the motive for Morrow's breakout, read excerpts from his letters to the red-haired woman. They were full of his passion for her. "Darling," the district attorney intoned, "you remind me of the Duchess of Alba." Morrow stared at the defense table as the letters were read.

He did not lift his eyes when Mrs. Shofner took the stand to testify. At one point the district attorney asked her, "Did he say anything before he died?"

Mrs. Shofner had been testifying calmly, but now her voice broke. "Yes," she almost whispered. "He said, 'Honey . . . I love you so much . . . .'"

Morrow, the romantic, squirmed in his chair.

On Death Row Morrow talked little. He didn't deny his guilt, offered no excuses, made no pleas. He walked through the little green door and shook his head when Warden H.E. Moore asked if he had anything to say. The guards strapped him to the chair and placed the mask on his face.

Suddenly a door to the chamber's outer court flew open. A man rushed into the Death House. He pushed through the witnesses, hurdled the iron railing, raced past the warden and the startled guards. He grasped the green curtain and pulled it back, exposing the executioner at his control board.

The man shouted, "There's the real murderer! There he is!"

Warden Moore took the man's shoulder and pulled the curtain from his grasp. He rearranged the curtain, then gently pushed the man into the hands of waiting guards. "Take him out," he said calmly. The man did not resist. He seemed surprised to find himself in the Death House.

Morrow, not seeing or understanding what was going on, was fighting his bonds. Warden Moore walked over to the chair. "It's nothing, Brazos," he said easily. "We're sorry."

Morrow relaxed—and died.

The intruder was a guard—one who had worked in the Death House until he had been assigned another post because of his growing distaste for the job.

The incident caused a change in the Death House. The executioner's switches were moved into a tiny adjoining room and he thereafter caught his signals from the warden through a one-way mirror.

Both of these men went down long before the fine rehabilitation programs were installed in the prison system.

Still thinking about them, I walked over to the prison and sought out Dr. Murray and her cool reasonableness. I told her everything I knew about West and Morrow, and somewhat embarrassed asked her, "If the programs had been in operation when they first hit prison, could they have been helped? Helped enough to . . . ?"

She nodded. "I feel sure they would have turned out differently."

She summoned Chris Tracy, who is in charge of testing and special projects for the school district. Tracy outlined all of the tests the men would have taken that would have revealed their attitudes, aptitudes and personality deviations. "Results of the tests would have told us where to assign the men—the groups they would fit in best with the least amount of conflict and the highest opportunity for success. We would have tried to discover their potentials and planned their futures."

Eventually West and Morrow would have wound up in one of the three programs developed by the school district —academic, vocational or creative. The purpose of the academic program, as I have written, is to teach the ignorant to read and write, add and subtract, knowledge vital to survival in the free world. The vocational program could have provided West and Morrow with skills to earn a living. The "esthetic" program frankly was devised to relieve frustrations of inmates. In this program art, dance and music are studied. Brazos Morrow would have loved the music course and perhaps the art. And he had brains enough to have become highly skilled at a trade. Nolan West could have learned how to make a living. Both, in my opinion, would not have killed, nor have been killed by the state.

11

Thoughts in Winter

I have been a newspaperman too long to hold any illusions about Americans *en masse*. If a reporter stopped a hundred adults on the sidewalk of any American city, save Washington, D.C., and asked each of them to identify Dean Rusk, say, no more than a dozen could properly do so. Inevitably, one among the dozen would say, "Oh yes! That's the guy with LBJ whose daughter married a black guy out in California!"

Americans *en masse* can be turned away from reality by a slogan, as evidenced by our political campaigns, and particularly if the slogan is an emotional one. The demands of daily living make analytical thought well-nigh impossible for a majority. And literate nation though we may be, these same demands limit our reading and make retention a sometime thing. So, in most instances, we think with our bellies. That 57 percent of those polled favored capital punishment for murder—after the Supreme Court decision—was no surprise to me.

Murder, of course, is a frightening thing. The citizen looks around to find someone on whom to place the blame for the large number of homicides annually. He picks up the handy phrases: "permissiveness," "undisciplined kids" and, for that matter, even "no respect for authority." Oftentimes he blames the police and the "criminal-coddling" prosecutors and judges.

But police, prosecutors and judges know something they seldom utter: murder is more a social problem than a criminal one. An FBI study of murder in the U.S. drew this conclusion: "The significant fact emerges that most murders are committed by the relatives of the victim or persons acquainted with the victim. It follows, therefore, that criminal homicide is, *to a major extent,* a national social problem *beyond police prevention.*"

But murder is not a social problem only because it is largely a "family affair." "Society" is all of us—but a majority of us determines what "society" does. And society refuses to provide some of us our rights and benefits, or protect them for us, while demanding the right to inflict cruel and unusual punishment on us when we strike out in ignorance, poverty and desperation bordering on insanity.

Perhaps society can never find a way to keep a long-suffering but suddenly enraged wife from slaying her husband, a jealous, drunken husband from slaying his wife. But society most certainly can alleviate if not eradicate the poverty, ignorance and injustice responsible for many of the murders outside the family group. From its record, society lacks the will. A few men have pushed it into accomplishing what has been done so far. There will be others like them, of course, but their lack of numbers makes the progress slow indeed.

Am I bitter? I think not. Cynical, yes, but cynicism never completely erases optimism. It bludgeons hope unmercifully but does not kill it. It does show one the possible.

Many of those who hold that capital punishment or the threat of it will stay a man from murder also maintain that capital punishment or threat of it deters men from committing lesser crimes as well. The late J. Edgar Hoover professed to be of such a mind. I say "professed" because I could never accept that he actually believed a thought of capital punishment ever entered the mind of a thief or burglar anymore than it entered the mind of a spouse driven over the edge of madness by a mate's excesses. The statistics he loved so much denied him the belief, if common sense didn't do so.

Hoover knew—as does anyone who has made a serious

study of crime—that the greatest deterrent to crime would be the absolute conviction that punishment for an illegal act would be swift and certain. Any illegal act committed by any sane citizen, of any color, of any social stratum. Society does not demand that punishment for *all* sane offenders be swift and certain—and we do not deter. We may never demand it, and we may never deter.

We do not deter, and we move slowly to alleviate the conditions that breed crime.

What is left is the possible—something we know we can do. We can reduce crimes, perhaps even murder and rape, by installing in our prison systems rehabilitation programs which will cut recidivism to its irreducible minimum. What the Texas prison system had done with its programs establishes that beyond doubt. And the Texas prison system can do better still—much better. The rewards for the effort would be both social and financial. The idea begets a slogan: safer streets for less money.

Illinois and Arkansas have studied the Texas example and are prepared to follow it. Ohio and New Jersey have been interested enough to examine the Texas programs. Other states have indicated a desire to study them. If the programs work as well elsewhere as they have in Texas— and there's no reason to doubt they will—a wholesome trend will be in the making.

I have not mentioned gun control before now simply because it seems impossible to obtain. Any literate adult should know that outlawing handguns would sharply reduce the murder rate—and that alone outweighs the hysterical tirades of the Nation Rifle Association and the calculated utterances of their financial supporters, the arms manufacturers. Both groups know better than most that the handgun, because it is so easily utilized, is the weapon used in more than fifty percent of the murders committed each year. It is the weapon the outraged father-in-law races to his bedroom to grab to kill the ornery son-in-law. The handgun lies on a low-hanging shelf to remind the jealous suitor that his rival cannot outrun a bullet. The robber cherishes it because it can be concealed until he wants to unveil it; he would rob less—and kill less—if he had to tote a rifle or a shotgun into the bank or liquor store.

So I advocate not the control of handguns by licensing or other half-measures but the restricting of their manufacture to the very few needed by police and other law enforcement agencies. I am aware, of course, that the Gun Lobby is so powerful that the Congress will not oppose its wishes, immoral as they may be. Morality, it seems at times, is not a major concern in Washington.

Just recently a veteran Liverpool policeman, Eric Simpson, visited my area. Liverpool is a city of about 2,000,000. In 1972, Simpson said, there were two murders in Liverpool and both were solved. Liverpool police do not carry firearms. Neither do the citizens, if the government can help it. Simpson said, "In eighteen years of police work I have never felt insecure because of not having a firearm. I'm not suggesting that a criminal cannot get hold of a gun. He can—but it is extremely hard for anyone to get anything but a hunting weapon."

Even more recently I was in London to appear on a David Frost television program about capital punishment. Supporters of capital punishment were making an annual effort to get the death sentence reinstated in England, and President Nixon a few days earlier had broadcast a message to Americans asking for its restoration. The Manchester *Guardian* published an editorial critical of both. Of Nixon, the editorial said in part: "His broadcast was filled with specious arguments and banal logic, but as a political tactic it may well improve the President's popularity. Mr. Nixon declared his belief in the deterrent effect of capital punishment in spite of the U.S. study which showed that no more policemen were killed in states where the death penalty has been abolished than in states where it was in force. He refused to accept the influence of social causes, in spite of the statistics which show that murder and violent crime are predominantly an urban problem which rises in proportion to the amount of decay, poverty and overcrowding in a community . . . ." In London, a city as large as New York, the editorial explained, the most recent annual statistics showed that police faced "real or imitation guns on only 20 occasions last year; the use of firearms was down from 387 to 380; and the combined total for murder, manslaughter and infanticide in 1972 was down by five to 113—which is just about the *weekly rate for New York City . . . .*"

On the Frost television show I declared that murderers are generally model prisoners, and seldom are recidivists. The reason, I explained, is because murderers in a majority of cases are what the experts call "situational" offenders— they know the person they kill—a relative or someone with whom they are well acquainted. I did not mention murderers in relation to rehabilitation programs, but after the show another panel member challenged me. He was a man of the cloth. He was irritated that I had suggested, or so he wrongly thought, that a killer could be rehabilitated. "You just don't change him," he said firmly. "He doesn't change his spots."

"Paul was a killer—and a competent one at that," I said. "Paul was a saint. Next to Christ himself as a force for Christianity."

My challenger stared at me a moment. Then, "Paul, yes," he said, nodding. "Good man, Paul." He walked out of the little office where he had detained me.

If capital punishment is not efficacious, is there a benign alternative? Yes, there is. It is life imprisonment. Not life imprisonment without hope of parole. Men without hope can and do make shambles of prison discipline and prison security. They stand not as an example to avoid, but rather as a reminder to other prisoners of man's continuing inhumanity to man. Their hopelessness floats over a prison the way the blues float through a nightclub from Duke Ellington's piano. There are no "good" prisoners among them. A man's conduct in prison most often is based on the degree of hope in his heart. For hope he needs a goal or goals. Give him a "freedom date" to work toward and his hope will sustain him though the date be half a century away. Give him a date, an effective rehabilitation program and an environment fit only for the meanest of free men and he may return to the city or farm with as much character and morality as the majority of us.

In this regard, only the judge should set the penalty for an offender in a major case. He should do this only after a pre-sentencing investigation by an independent authority composed of a capable investigator, a psychiatrist and a citizen reasonable men would consider honest and competent. Not always does a jury hear *all* of the information available in a case. Prosecutors withhold evidence favorable to the defendant, defense lawyers withhold evidence damaging to the defendant. As we have seen in previous chapters, defense attorneys too often present no evidence at all in a defendant's behalf. A judge can command all of this information. The pre-sentencing investigatory group can learn the background of a case, including actions and motivations of both the accused and the victim. So armed, a judge can make an intelligent penalty judgment.

Some argue that a Grand Jury performs this pre-sentencing service. This is rank nonsense. A Grand Jury hears only enough evidence to determine whether an indictment or a no-bill should be returned—enough to order that a proper trial be held or the case forgotten. In too many instances a Grand Jury hears only what a district attorney wants to tell it, and every aware attorney knows it.

Sometimes after I make a speech a listener will bring up the "sanctity of life" and argue that a man should be executed if he violates this sanctity. It is a pallid argument, and it destroys itself. If an individual should not disregard the sanctity of life, neither should the state. If a man kills in blind anger, we execute him. If he drives his car through a stop sign and kills a child, we do not.

So much for the sanctity of life.

It appears almost ironic that as I am writing these words lawmen in several nearby counties have dug up the bodies of almost thirty youths who were tortured, sexually abused and murdered by a 33-year-old homosexual psychopath who himself was slain by one of two young accomplices. It is a crime of such magnitude that the mind can hardly grasp and accept it.

Already I sense a tiny groundswell of compassion for the two youths. Houston police obviously have violated several of the youths' legal rights, but I don't believe that is responsible for the groundswell of compassion I sense. Perhaps it is because the public feels the youths were lured into the terrible activities by the psychopath.

But what if this man had not been killed? There would have been no compassion for him. The thought of what he did sends a shudder through the body. Instinctively, we would have wanted to cry out, "Kill him like the mad dog he is!" Indeed, we are angered because he is beyond our reach.

How, then, can I write that this vicious being should not have been electrocuted had he survived?

For one thing, he was insane, and to judge him as we would judge ourselves would be legally impermissible and morally reprehensible. Knowing this, to execute him would be an act of pure revenge without a shadow of justice to modify the act. To execute him would be an admission that we did so only to dispose of him without thought of any of the saving graces on which civilization, such as it is, was built.

And we cannot isolate this case anymore than we can isolate the case of Lieutenant William Calley, who was responsible for even more deaths of innocents than the homosexual psychopath. I can more easily comprehend the actions of the psychopath than understand the more calculated actions of Lieutenant Calley, who was presumed sane, but I didn't and don't want Calley executed. I didn't want him to become a political issue, either. In compassion for him, I wanted him thoroughly examined by nonpolitical psychiatrists, and a rehabilitation program devised for him that offered hope of parole at a time when and if he were prepared to rejoin society. For the psychopath I would have hoped for incarceration of at least two-thirds of his life expectancy before he would be *considered for parole*, and then only after psychiatric treatment had been administered to the satisfaction of experts in the prison and the court.

to the satisfaction of experts in the prison and the court.

We cannot isolate any case simply because it is an exception to the rule. We live by the rule, not the exception. Under the law, a man who murders one man is as guilty as if he had murdered a dozen in one swoop. If we give him the electric chair for one murder, we would not boil him in oil for a dozen. If we maintain life imprisonment as the maximum punishment for murder, we should not cry out that it is a failure because now and then some particularly sensational crime arouses our excitement and tribal bloodlust. The sensational crime, as we now know, is the exception to the rule . . . and the exception must be understood for what it is. If I can not condone capital punishment for the "family affair" murders, the killings that result from hot-headed arguments and those which are spawned by ignorance and deprivation, I will not condone it for the comparatively rare exceptions.

In these scores of pages I have written of attitudes I held, people I met and events I witnessed and participated in over a 35-year period. I have no difficulty recalling the people and the events; my memories of them are sharp and accurate, and my memories are aided by bales of notes, books of newspaper clippings and stacks of wire recordings and tape recordings. It has been harder to recall my changing attitudes as I matured and, I think, grew a bit wiser. I have done the best I could.

As you know, I was no "bleeding heart" when first I came to Huntsville and began covering the prison system. It took witnessing a great number of executions over a number of years before I began questioning an establishment practice. More time and a great amount of study followed before I accepted as clear-cut fact that capital punishment was administered inequitably, unwisely and, in truth, failed to accomplish what it had been designed to do—deter.

Even then it took a change of attitude before I mounted my charger and sallied forth to do battle against what I still consider an unmitigated evil.

At the age of 66, I became publisher-emeritus of the *Item* in August of 1973. I still write for the paper, and hope to do so until I die. But I no longer bear the other pleasant burdens of management. In these winter years I look forward like other men to the delights my age affords me. But I have fought too long against capital punishment and other injustices to lay aside my armor or even burnish it for viewing only. As a former President once told a pre-election throng, "I am an old campaigner, and I love a good fight . . . ."

12

The Last Ride

It was, for a wonder, a cool July night. The night of July 29, 1964. At midnight a 29-year-old black, Joseph Johnson, Jr., was scheduled to ride "Old Sparky." Because of the many recent court decisions, because of the decreasing number of men dying in Death Houses across the land, I had a feeling, nothing more, that tonight's ritual would be the last celebrated inside the walls I was approaching in my car.

I was early. In the bright moonlight the vine-covered walls seemed more appropriate to a splendid estate than a prison. I parked near the front gate. I waved to the guard in his cubicle atop the wall and started up the entrance steps. But I had mounted only a few steps when I paused. It was too early to go inside . . . the night too lovely.

I lit a cigar and began strolling along the wall, savoring the night. My path led me to an old road that stretched past the rear of the prison. I came at last, without conscious volition, to where a sandy knoll rose up in the moonlight. Peckerwood Hill, inmates and natives alike called it. It is the burial ground for the remains of men and women prisoners whose bodies had not been claimed by relatives or friends. Many of those who died in the electric chair are here because they died in the time before the Texas Medical Center in Houston began using the bodies of executed men for study purposes.

It is a neat cemetery, well-kept, and the rows of gray headstones seem to march across the top of the knoll. The night was so bright I could see the numbers on them. No names. The unclaimed dead of the Texas prison system are remembered by numbers only.

My steps turned toward a fence surrounding one plot near the top of the knoll. This was the grave of Chief Red Wing, the only Indian formally executed by the State of Texas. Red Wing was a member of an Oklahoma tribe. During his trial for murder in Comal County he had used a Mexican name, and his attorney had tried to pass him off as a Mexican national and immune to U.S. laws. After his burial on Peckerwood Hill, several members of his tribe came down from Oklahoma and erected the fence. Later they returned and claimed the chief's body for interment in the tribal burial grounds. They left the gravesite fenced in, and it was never disturbed.

I turned in the direction of the prison gate. Peckerwood Hill now has an official name—The Joe Byrd Memorial Cemetery—so designated by the prison system in memory of Joe Byrd, the baggy-trousered long-time assistant warden and executioner. If the system saw anything ironic in its choice of names, it was never voiced. Byrd, after his retirement and before his death, spent many hours in the cemetery. He saw to it that graves were cared for, that flowers grew above the bodies resting there. He knew the names of many of the men beneath the numbers, Joe Byrd did. I often wondered what his thoughts must have been as he worked there, if some strange compulsion sent him there each day as surely as he had gone to work inside the prison before his retirement.

But he went there, and he poured loving care on that resting place. And he remembered. As the woman from Virginia wrote in her letter about that "odd man," William Henry Meyer: "Immortality is somebody remembering some-one . . . ."

Joseph Johnson handed me a note before he walked through the little green door. He had written: "I offer my life to God, from whence it came, that the Negro people receive equal rights and that there is harmony between the races . . . ."

Earlier he had insisted quietly that he was visiting a friend and watching television on the night of the murder for which he had been convicted. No one in authority had believed him, and the evidence that he had killed a Chinese grocer in a robbery-shootout was overwhelming.

He entered the Death House at 12:02 a.m. He was carrying a white Bible. He asked for and was granted permission to kneel and pray. "Oh God, have mercy on these people," he intoned. "Have mercy on me, and bless these people."

He died with the Bible in his lap. When the electricity shocked him, the Bible spun from his lap with such speed that it landed in the witness area. The doctor pronounced him dead at 12:08 a.m., July 30, 1964.

In the story I filed to the Associated Press, I speculated correctly, as it turned out—that Johnson's execution would be the last in Huntsville. I went home. I was desperately weary and shaken when I got in bed and went to sleep.

Someone pushed me through a door and I was standing in the Death House; I looked around. There was the warden, the chaplain, the doctor. There were strangers standing in the witness area where I always had stood before. Guards were at my side; it had been the guards who had pushed me through the door. I was puzzled, and I felt that my bewilderment should be evident to those silent faces. Then the warden spoke—and I felt the beginning of fear.

"Do you have anything to say, Don?" he asked softly.

"Of course I don't! Why in the hell should I say something?" I looked around wildly, but only the unsmiling faces fell in my line of vision.

"Have a seat, please," the warden said, still softly.

I stared at him. He gestured toward the electric chair. He moved his head to indicate that I should sit down.

"Are you crazy?" My voice was loud and shrill in the Death House. "What are you doing? You know me! I'm Don Reid! We've known each other for years! Haven't we always been friends?" My body was shaking. I was

being torn apart by fear and rage and a sense of helplessness that made me want to weep. "Why don't you stop this!" I screamed.

He shook his head soberly. "I'm sorry, Don. You know there is nothing I can do. You're next . . . ."

I was standing by my bed, bathed in sweat, screaming hysterically, and the world was spinning away from me. Then I realized Frances was beside me, her hands caressing my shoulders, her voice murmuring its way into my consciousness. "It's only a dream, Darling," she murmured over and over . . . "only a dream . . . ."

Don Reid spent thirty-five years covering the Texas prison system for the *Huntsville Item* and Associated Press. During his illustrious career, he became a major national spokesman for the abolition of the death penalty.

Reid began his newspaper career on the *Tribune* in Chicago, where he covered the underworld beat during the bloodiest chapter of that city's history. After moving back to Texas and working briefly with the McAllen *Monitor*, Reid came to Huntsville, where he eventually served as editor and finally publisher-emeritus of the *Huntsville Item*.